Reading Roadmaps

A Literary Scope & Sequence for K-12

by
Adam & Missy Andrews

Table of Contents

How To Use This Book

Reading Roadmaps helps teachers apply the *Teaching the Classics* method of literary analysis in the classroom . It is first and foremost a Scope & Sequence manual, offering annotated reading lists for grades K-12, specially chosen for use with *Teaching the Classics*. More than 200 titles have been selected, summarized and cross-referenced with the elements of fiction common to all stories. After completing their own reading, teachers can prepare for their classes in just a few minutes by glancing at a chart that summarizes plot, conflict, theme and literary devices for each week's reading. Alternate titles for every entry allow teachers to adjust reading assignments to fit their own preferences. Best of all, *Reading Roadmaps* ensures that your students will encounter some of the best loved classics of Western literature and be well prepared, both for college and for life in the wide world.

We understand that every homeschool family is unique in its approach and emphasis. While some make classic books the central focus of their instruction, others address literature occasionally, granting more time to math and science. *Reading Roadmaps* also helps you adapt the *Teaching the Classics* method to your particular situation, regardless of how much time you decide to devote to literature. Several scope and sequence models allow you to provide effective lit classes on a frequent or infrequent basis. For example, if Literature is your highest priority or if you are a classroom lit teacher, the Daily/Weekly Model will work for you. If on the other hand you're a Math/Science mom who wants to provide no more than a brief exposure to Lit, perhaps the Seasonal Model is best.

Scope & Sequence Models: Chapters 1 through 5

In order to use this book properly, first decide how often you plan to conduct in-depth lit classes with your students (keeping in mind that in order to conduct these classes, you'll have to read the books too). Then choose the Scope & Sequence model that best fits your needs according to the following chart:

If you plan to conduct a class:	Turn to chapter:
Every day or once a week	Two (the Daily/Weekly Model)
Once a month	Three (the Monthly Model)
Every six weeks or so	Four (the Six-week Model)
Five times a year	Five (the Quarterly Model)
Four times a year	Six (the Seasonal Model)

(If you decide to conduct fewer than three formal discussions in a year, use the Seasonal Model and simply omit the last title or two.)

Once you've chosen a model, turn to the corresponding chapter and begin. There's no need to consult the other models. The recommended reading lists, annotations and study aids are adapted specifically for you.

The Roadmaps

Each scope and sequence model contains a complete set of reading charts, or "Roadmaps" – one for each grade level from K-12. These charts present a sequential reading list for an entire academic year based on the selected model. For each title in the list, the Roadmap provides the following information in an easy to read layout:

- The story's place in the yearly schedule
- The story's title and author
- A summary of the story's basic Plot
- A list of important Conflicts driving the story
- An identification of major Themes in the story
- A list of Stylistic Devices used in the story, if applicable
- A link to Center For Lit study aids specific to the story, if applicable
- An alternate story selection

In addition, the introduction to each set of Roadmaps provides specific instructions for daily and weekly lesson plans appropriate to that model.

Supplementary Material: Chapters 6 through 10

The supplementary materials in chapters 6 through 10 will help you with a variety of topics related to teaching Literature. You'll learn how to assign and grade literary analysis essays in chapter 6, "Writing from literature." Chapter 7 offers a grade-by-grade summary of objectives for teachers who want a standard by which to judge their students' progress. In chapter 8, *Reading Roadmaps* covers the important subject of Grading and Credits, showing you a simple way to quantify and evaluate your students' work and assemble report cards and transcripts. It even includes reproducible grade sheets for your use. Chapter 9 gives a timeline of major periods in the history of Western literature, complete with a description of the ruling ideas of each period and a list of important authors and their major works.

For further assistance, please visit CenterForLit online at www.centerforlit.com, or email Adam Andrews (adam@centerforlit.com) or Missy Andrews (missy@centerforlit.com).

Chapter 1

The Daily/Weekly Model

The Daily/Weekly Model

The Daily/Weekly Model is intended for educators pursuing an intensive study of literature through daily or weekly classes. This model allows the most extensive treatment of the books themselves. With this model, teachers should have plenty of time not only to simply identify basic elements of plot and literary devices, but also to extensively treat these elements, reading passages aloud, dwelling on individual devices and their presence in the text, and doing extension projects that involve other content based subjects such as writing, history, science and other subjects.

A basic lesson plan for the Daily/Weekly model depends largely on the grade level in question. Kindergarten and first grade classes will apply the model differently than second through twelfth grade classes.

Kindergarten and First Grade:

Teaching the Classics is a literature program rather than a phonics program. Because of this, kindergarten and first graders should be engaged in phonics instruction beyond this program. The titles on the kindergarten reading list, 36 main titles and 36 alternates, allow up to two titles per week in a given 36 week school year. Most kindergarten classrooms employ daily read aloud time. In these classrooms, the teacher may choose to utilize one title per week, rereading and addressing various extension subjects as encountered, or two titles per week in the same fashion. (This approach is advocated by Claire Lambert in her popular series, *5 In A Row*.) For those teachers addressing one book weekly, the second list of titles may be used as alternates to accommodate teacher preference.

For the first few weeks of the school year, the teacher should spend a full week on each element of story as presented in the *Teaching the Classics* basic seminar. For example, in week 1 the teacher will read a story and introduce the idea of setting. In week 2, she may read the second story and introduce the element of character. With the story in week 3, the idea of conflict may be presented, with the plot chart occupying the discussions in weeks 4 and 5. In week 6, the teacher may present the idea of theme, suggesting possible themes associated with the previous stories read in class to illustrate the concept.

By week 7, students should be ready in a discussion context to apply what they've learned in order to identify the elements of story in the remaining books they encounter throughout the school year. If the teacher is using the <u>Weekly</u> Model, the class will identify all story elements (setting, characters, plot, conflict, theme, literary devices) for the week's selection in a single session. If the teacher is using the <u>Daily</u> Model, the following sample weekly lesson plan is applicable to weeks 7 through 36:

> **Weekly Schedule – Daily Model:**
>
> - Monday – Read the story aloud for enjoyment and identify any literary devices that apply.

- Tuesday – Reread the story and discuss setting and characters.
- Wednesday – Reread the story and discuss conflict.
- Thursday – Reread the story and discuss the plot, creating a plot chart together as a class on the board.
- Friday – Reread the story and discuss possible themes.

Should the teacher wish to employ extension art projects or tie-ins with other content based subjects, this lesson plan can be truncated, addressing more story elements each day to free Friday for other projects.

Because the primary goal of literature in kindergarten is to expose children to story and foster a love for reading, reading aloud to them is singularly important. What you "do with a book" is a lesser question. Teaching a child to enjoy reading involves teaching them to sit still and to listen. Of course, discipline may be required to accomplish this with some. Don't be discouraged by this. It is a necessary part of the process of teaching a child, and at this stage it is perhaps the most important thing the child must learn. If a child won't respect authority, if he/she can't sit still and focus for any given period of time, education cannot take place. It's impossible to teach an untrained child.

In addition, since the love of reading supersedes any program goals for kindergarteners, **the teacher need not feel pressure to fully treat every story presented to the children throughout the year**. Feel free to truncate lessons, presenting a single element of story to the class if desired. At times, the instructor may choose only to read the story, rather than to discuss it fully. That's fine. The important thing is that teachers be reading aloud regularly and using literary terminology to refer to story parts.

First graders will employ the same basic model as kindergarteners. However, first graders may enjoy practicing their reading aloud in class using some of the titles provided. For this purpose, the first grade list includes a multitude of readers such as the Henry and Mudge series and the Amelia Bedelia books. Should the teacher choose to do the entire course as student read-alouds, the class will encounter fewer titles over the course of the year. This is entirely up to the educator. The application of this course is infinitely flexible to accommodate individual classrooms and students.

Second Grade:

The second grade reading list is much shorter. By the second grade, students should be approaching reading more and more independently. Titles included for second graders are beginning chapter book readers. Some of these are episodic in nature, each chapter presenting a complete short story. Other books present a longer story in chapter format. Books should be treated accordingly, with episodic books applying story analysis to individual chapters. The model assumes students are reading aloud to one another in a classroom environment; therefore, the list allows for 1-2 chapters per week. Should this prove ambitious, teachers may choose to do some of the reading aloud themselves to allow ample time for discussion. Again, second grade is a kind of transition year with students working towards reading independence. Educators should be employing a phonics curriculum since phonics instruction is outside the scope of this curriculum.

Each story on the second grade list requires 3-5 weeks for instruction. Students will read and treat a total of 8 titles in a given academic year. Should the teacher wish, she might utilize titles from the first grade list to do more reading aloud to the students. Since the teacher is probably treating other subjects such as history, science, etc., story analysis may be applied to longer stories that the teacher is reading to the students in these other subjects. In either case, the same treatment of story would apply.

Here is a model lesson plan for second grade that works for both the Daily and Weekly models:

- Week 1-2 – Students read aloud the first two chapters and discuss setting and character.
- Weeks 3-4 – Students read chapters 3-4 and discuss conflict and plot, beginning a plot chart as a class.
- Week 5 – Students complete the reading and the plot chart to discuss theme.

For shorter books, story elements may be presented as they are encountered. Literary devices, too, should be taught as they are encountered in the reading. Remember to identify each story by genre, as well, so as to teach the kids to recognize the different types of literature. An alternate list of books is provided to allow for teacher preferences.

Third through Twelfth Grade:

Third through twelfth graders should be reading independently, rather than in the classroom. Each list begins with 4 children's picture storybook selections. These are included to allow teachers to reintroduce in review fashion the 5 elements of story and the plot chart. If the class has never used the *Teaching the Classics* model, the teacher should use these stories to introduce the structural parts of a story, highlighting one or two elements at a time to equip the students for longer discussions of the selections at their grade level. Grade level selections number 8 titles per academic year.

With the Daily Model, the teacher should be able to cover the picture books in one week, reviewing story elements and preparing students for the larger work of discussing books at their own grade level. Of course, if the teacher feels students need more time to assimilate the analytical model, additional time of up to 4 full weeks may be allowed. Teachers using the Weekly Model will want to focus on picture books for several weeks at least. More picture book titles are available in the kindergarten and first grade lists. Don't hesitate to employ them. Some are better than others for use with older students. Take a moment to look them up if you are unfamiliar with the titles. Choose stories rich in theme for discussion with older students. Many of these "children's" books aren't really for children at all!

Once the teacher feels the model for analysis has been adequately introduced, he should begin the titles from the main reading list, allowing 4-5 weeks per book title. If the initial picture books were addressed in the course of a single week, the remaining three weeks allotted for introductory teaching may be used to lengthen reading and discussion time as needed for the study of other books over the course of the year. Should the teacher take the full four weeks to introduce the analytical model, each subsequent title on the main list will receive 4 weeks for treatment. Here is a sample yearly schedule for both Daily and Weekly Models:

Yearly Lesson Schedule:

Week 1 – Introduce the elements of character and setting in story using picture book #1.

Week 2 – Introduce the elements of conflict and plot using picture book #2.

Week 3 – Using picture book #3, plot the story on a plot chart, identifying setting, character, and conflict. Stress that the climax of the story is connected with the motivations of the main character, anticipating a resolution of one of the story's important conflicts.

Week 4 – Using picture book #4, plot the story on a plot chart, identifying setting, character and conflict. Introduce the concept of themes, underlying ideas and universal thoughts that encompass the story's message.

Week 5 – Begin the first title on your main list. Allow one week for pre-reading. At the end of week one, lead a discussion on elements of setting and initial character development.

Week 6 – Student should continue reading. Continue to address elements of character and setting, looking to identify the major conflict in the story. This is usually introduced in the first quarter of the book.

Week 7 – Student should be nearly finished with the reading. Continue the discussion of conflict in order to arrive at a discussion of plot elements. Plot the story on a plot chart, taking time to discuss various possible plot climax points.

Week 8 – This week, discussion should treat the various themes within the story, with an eye to the fact that theme and conflict are intimately connected to one another. Depending on the grade level, the teacher may want to give an end of study test. This may be given at the week's end. The teacher should assign a writing extension of some sort to cap off the unit. This may be a thematic essay, a creative writing extension, or a descriptive essay dealing with one of the story elements. That is to say, this may be a creative writing assignment, an expository essay, or a persuasive thematic essay depending on the age and abilities of the students. (See chapter 7 for more information on writing from literature.) Younger students may benefit from doing a report on a subject related to the story. For example, third graders reading *Misty of Chincoteague* may benefit from a research report on the ponies of Assateague Island and Pony Penning Day, or more simply on the subject of horses. Give students 2-3 weeks to write and edit papers. Papers should go through at the very least a rough draft and one edit. Two edits may prove more fruitful. Obviously, this means that the student will be writing his/her essay on the previous book while reading and discussing the next assigned book. Deal with these writing assignments in a different hour (a writing class), or in individual appointments with the students (preferred). Some children enjoy doing extension projects. This would be the place for arts and crafts! (You know the drill: popsicle log cabins, miniatures, dioramas, drawings/paintings, etc. The sky is the limit. Be creative. We once had a student become so inspired by *The Indian in the Cupboard* that he built a miniature log house like one Omri's Indian made!)

Week 9 – 12 - Begin the 2nd selection. Repeat the model throughout the year.

Week 13-16 – Book 3

Week 17-20 – Book 4

Week 21-24 – Book 5

Week 25-28 – Book 6

Week 29-32 – Book 7

Week 33-36 – Book 8

While teachers using the Weekly Model will of course accomplish each week's goal in a single session, those using the Daily Model may use the following schedule for best results:

Weekly Lesson Schedule – Daily Model:

Weeks 1-4

In weeks 1-4, when children's books are indicated on the Roadmap, the teacher may wish to discuss each selection in full over the course of a week, treating setting, characters, plot, conflict, theme and literary devices on successive days. For older students already familiar with the Teaching the Classics model, all 4 books may be covered in a single week to review and practice the model. This will free up weeks 2-4, allowing more time for the study of lengthier selections later in the year.

Week 5: Begin the first grade level selection, employing the Socratic List

Monday – Tuesday	Initial contextual information is given by teacher to the students. Any historical information regarding the setting of the story or the background of the author may be introduced here.
Wednesday	Silent reading in class.
Thursday – Friday	Initial discussion of the setting and any literary devices encountered in reading.

Week 6

Monday – Tuesday	Complete the discussion of setting and begin a discussion of characters.
Wednesday	Silent reading in class.

| Thursday – Friday | Utilize class time to list and describe qualities of major characters. Give expository writing assignments concerning characters within the story. If time allows, help students with writing efforts in class. Introduce any literary devices encountered in reading this week. |

Week 7

Monday-Tuesday	Discuss conflicts and plot developments.
Wednesday	Silent reading in class.
Thursday	Assign a plot chart to students as homework. Allow them to work on it in class.
Friday	Collect student plot charts, then plot the story on the board in class, distinguishing the pivotal, climactic moment. Discuss students' various opinions concerning this. Introduce any literary devices encountered in reading this week.

Week 4

Monday	Finish plotting the story, dealing with the denouement and conclusion. Hand out any study guides for the test.
Tuesday	Begin your discussion of themes. Assign thematic essays and writing extensions or any culminating projects.
Wednesday	Continue your discussion of theme. Introduce any final literary elements encountered in week's reading.
Thursday	In class help getting started with papers. Thesis/Outline help.
Friday	Final Exam

In order for students to be able to complete the plot chart assignment by the end of week 3, they will need to have completed the reading of the book in its entirety. This is ambitious in the secondary grades, and assumes that students will have ample time to read on a daily basis.

All discussions should be led using the Socratic method as described in the *Teaching the Classics* basic seminar. A list of questions to aid in discussion may be found in the appendix of the *Teaching the Classics* syllabus. The questions are graded in nature, organized in increasing order of complexity within each listed story element. The questions are generic and may consequently be applied to the study of any story.

Kindergarten

Week	Title	Plot
1	*The Runaway Bunny,* Brown	A bunny asserts his independence by repeatedly running away from his mother, only to find that she is everywhere he goes.
2	*The Hungry Caterpillar,* Carle	A caterpillar eats his way through the groceries, fueling up for his grand transformation.
3	*The Water Hole,* Baese	Animals of the savannah learn the value of water when their water hole dries up.
4	*Olivia,* Falconer	Precocious Olivia entertains readers with her antics and ingenuity but wears her mother right out!
5	*The Poky Little Puppy,* Lowrey	The Poky Little Puppy repeatedly disregards his mother's words and loses his dessert privileges.
6	*The Bee Tree,* Polacco	A reluctant reader learns the sweetness of hard won success when her grandfather takes her on a bee hunt.
7	*The Bundle Book,* Krauss	A mother and her child play a guessing game.
8	*The Carrot Seed* , Krauss	A boy labors diligently to grow a carrot from a seed despite naysayers.
9	*The Tale of Peter Rabbit* , Potter	Peter disobeys his mother's order and sneaks into Mr. McGregor's garden, losing his new clothes and catching a terrible cold.
10	*Rainbow Fish* , Pfister	The lovely, rainbow-colored fish wins friends by sharing.
11	*The Story About Ping,* Flack	Duckling Ping, surfacing to find he's missed the call to return to his master, will surely be spanked, so he runs away.
12	*Blueberries for Sal* , McCloskey	Sal's mother takes her blueberry picking on the same day that a bear cub's mother takes HER blueberry picking!
13	*The Velveteen Rabbit* , Williams	When scarlet fever contaminates a boy's favorite stuffed bunny, magic transforms it into a real rabbit.
14	*If You Give a Mouse a Cookie* , Numeroff	When a boy befriends a mouse by giving him a cookie, he sets a circular chain of events in motion.
15	*Tough Boris* , Fox	Though a pirate bold a fierce, Boris mourns when his pet parrot dies.

Daily/Weekly Model

Conflict	Theme	Aids/Devices	Alternate Title	Week
Man vs. Man	Love is patient, perseverant, wise, unchangeable and unavoidable.	Repetition	*Dr. De Soto*, Steig	1
Man vs. Nature	Metamorphosis	Basic story elements	*Casey At the Bat,* retold by Polacco	2
Creature vs. Nature	Renewal, social interdependence	Repetition	*Blueberries for Sal*, McCloskey	3
Man vs. Man	Patience and Love	Understatement	*Tops and Bottoms*, Stevens	4
Man vs. Man	Consequences of disobedience	Repetition	*Each Peach, Pear, Plum,* Ahlsberg	5
Man vs. Nature, Man vs. Self	Rewards of patience and perseverance, the sweetness of success	Alliteration, Dialect, Symbolism	*Why Mosquitoes Buzz in People's Ears*, Aardema	6
None!	A playfull illustration of mother love	Basic story elements	*The Ox-Cart Man*, Hall	7
Man vs. Man	Patience, perseverance and faith	Understatement	*Old Henry*, Blos	8
Man vs. Man, Man vs. Nature	Consequences of disobedience	*Teaching the Classics* basic seminar	*The Tale of Benjamin Bunny*, Potter	9
Man vs. Self	Self-sacrifice, sharing	Circumstantial irony	*Just Plain Fancy*, Polacco	10
Man vs. Self	Responsibility-taking, facing consequences	Personification, Sensory Language	*Sky Boys*, Hopkinson	11
Man vs. Nature	Caution, paying attention	Sensory language	*The Magic Fan*, Baker	12
Man vs. Nature	The power of love, the meaning of "real;" self sacrifice; life coming out of death.	Symbolism	*The Emperor and the Kite*, Yolen	13
Man vs. Man, Man vs. Nature	Cause and Effect	Irony, understatement	*The Journey,* Stewart	14
Man vs. Nature	Everyone cries; the meaning of "tough;" manliness	Irony	*Babushka Baba Yaga*, Polacco	15

Week	Title	Plot
16	*Apples to Oregon* , Hopkinson	Daddy and Delicious embark on a journey from Iowa to Oregon with a "nursery" wagon full of fruit trees and hearts full of hope.
17	*Noah's Ark,* Spier	While a worldwide flood destroys the earth and its inhabitants, Noah and his family care for a floating zoo of animals, all safe in the ark God told him to build.
18	*Goldilocks and the Three Bears*	When a little girl enters a house uninvited, she sets herself up for a fright.
19	*The Little Red Hen* , Galdone	While the Red Hen's friends refuse to do the work of planting, tending, harvesting and processing wheat for bread, they are eager to eat the fruit of her labors.
20	*The Gingerbread Boy,* Galdone	The saucy gingerbread boy runs away from his creators, taunting them, but is outwitted at last by a sly fox.
21	*The Three Billy Goats Gruff,* Galdone	An ugly troll threatens three billy goat brothers who cross his bridge.
22	*The Bremen Town Musicians,* Grimm	Traveling animal musicians discover robbers in a house and trick them out of their ill-gotten gain.
23	*Are You My Mother?,* Eastman	While mother bird hunts for food for the baby chick that will soon hatch, the baby bird is born. In confusion, he sets out to find his mother.
24	*The Three Little Pigs* , original	Three piggy brothers set out to seek their fortunes, but are plagued by a wolf.
25	*The Three Little Pigs, retold,* Wiesner	The big, bad wolf blows Pig #1 right out of the pages of the story book where, inviting his brothers to join him, he ventures into the pages of other stories, making friends and outwitting his nemesis, the wolf.
26	*Red Riding Hood* , Grimm	A little girl disobeys her mother by straying from the path on the way to visit her grandma.
27	*Harriet, You'll Drive Me Wild,* Fox	Little Harriet doesn't mean to trouble her mother any more than her mother means to lose her temper, but when Harriet's childish mistakes snowball, both find themselves in need of forgiveness.
28	*The Princess and the Pea* , Cech	Aided by his mother and a pea, a prince finds a real princess
29	*Cinderella* , Rackham	An orphaned girl, abused by her stepmother and stepsisters, wins the heart of a handsome prince with the help of her fairy-godmother.
30	*Peter and the Wolf* , Prokofiev	When Peter goes beyond the garden gate, he is stalked by a ravenous wolf.

Conflict	Theme	Aids/Devices	Alternate Title	Week
Man vs. Nature	Determination, perseverance, cooperation, vision	*Ready Readers* at CenterForLit website	*King Bidgood's In the Bathtub* ,Wood	16
Man vs. God, Man vs. Nature, Man vs. Self	Salvation; Obedience to God	Rhyme, alliteration, understatement	*Bored, Nothing To Do* , Spier	17
Man vs. Nature, Man vs. Man	Private property, courtesy, theft	Anthropomorphism	*The Ugly Duckling* , Anderson	18
Man vs. Man, Man vs. Self	Laziness vs. Diligence	Anthropomorphism, repetition	*Sleeping Beauty,* Grimm	19
Man vs. Man, Man vs. Self	Consequences of arrogance and pride	Personification	*The Treasure* , Shulevitz	20
Man vs. Man, Good vs. Evil	Retributive Justice	Repetition, irony	*It Could Always Be Worse* , Zemach	21
Man vs. Man	Ill-gotten gain comes to no good.	Anthropomorphism, simile	*Hansel and Gretel* , Grimm	22
Man vs. Nature	The journey home	Repetition	*The Emperor's New Clothes* , Anderson	23
Man vs. Man	Diligence prospers; good vs. evil	Anthropomorphism, repetition	*The Princess and the Pea* , Anderson	24
Man vs. Man	Good vs. Evil	Circumstantial irony	*Rapunzel,* Grimm	25
Man vs. Nature, Man vs. Man	Consequences of disobedience	Foreshadowing	*Beauty and the Beast* , Grimm	26
Man vs. Man, Man vs. Self	Self-control, patience, repentance forgiveness and reconciliation	*Ready Readers* at CenterForLit website	*Alexander and the Terrible, Horrible, No Good, Very Bad Day,* Viorst	27
Man vs. Man	Appearance vs. reality, deception, trust	Symbolism, satire	*And To Think That I Saw It On Mulberry Street* , Seuss	28
Man vs. Man	Rewards of goodness, good vs. evil	Irony	*Thy Friend, Obadiah* , Turkle	29
Man vs. Nature	Man's dominion over nature	Anthropomorphism	*The Whispering Rabbit,* Brown	30

Week	Title	Plot
31	*The Little Engine that Could* , Piper	When their train's engine breaks down, some circus performers and dolls seek another engine to help them reach the children in the valley over the pass; only the littlest engine will help them.
32	*The Keeping Quilt* , Polacco	An immigrant family preserves its heritage and memories in a special keepsake: a quilt that becomes a family heirloom.
33	*The Mitten* , Brett	A boy's lost mitten becomes home to a plethora of forest creatures.
34	*A New Coat for Anna* , Ziefert	The war makes it difficult to get goods, but Anna's mother trades with her neighbors to provide a coat for her growing daughter.
35	*Corduroy* , Freeman	A small stuffed bear finds a home.
36	*The Money Tree,* Stewart	Miss McGillicuddy must decide how to handle the money tree that springs up unbidden in her yard, luring neighbors to greedy extremes.

Conflict	Theme	Aids/Devices	Alternate Title	Week
Man vs. Man	Perseverance, humility, helpfulness, kindness	Personification	*Ferdinand,* Lawson	31
Man vs. Nature	The preservation of heritage and family in the face of time's passage	Symbolism	*Thank You, Mr. Falker*, Polacco	32
Man vs. Self	Responsibility-taking	Imagery, Adjectives	*Stone Soup*, Brown	33
Man vs. Society	Patience, cooperation, value, free market economics	Alliteration, assonance	*Humble Pie*, Donnelly	34
Man vs. Self	Love, friendship	Personification	*Norman, the Doorman*, Freeman	35
Man vs. Self, Man vs. Society	Greed; contentment; human nature	Imagery	*Chicken Sunday*, Polacco	36

1ˢᵗ Grade

Week	Title	Plot
1	*The Story of Ferdinand,* Leaf	Unlike the other bulls, Ferdinand refuses to fight in the bullfights in Madrid, preferring peaceful contemplation in his meadow.
2	*Thunder Cake,* Polacco	Babushka decides to cure her granddaughter of cowardice by making her face some of her fears.
3	*Little Toot,* Gramatky	Little Toot lacks the gravity of his tugboat companions and father is critical of his figure-eight antics; but in a grave moment, Little Toot saves the day.
4	*Brave Irene,* Steig	When her seamstress mother is taken ill, young Irene braves a snowstorm to deliver a gown commissioned by the duchess.
5	*A Bargain for Frances,* Hoban	Frances, swindled by her friend Thelma, gets even.
6	*Squirrel Nutkin,* Potter	Rude Squirrel Nutkin learns some manners when he offends old Mr. Owl
7	*Amos and Boris,* Steig	The story of an unlikely friendship between a mouse and a whale reminiscient of Aesop's fable of the mouse and the lion.
8	*Madeline,* Bemelmans	Madeline, adept at scaring Miss Clavel, becomes the center of attention when she suffers acute appendicitis.
9	*Owl Moon,* Yolen	A father and child go owling in this coming of age classic.
10	*The Relatives Came,* Rylant	A child relates a visit from his relatives.
11	*The Treasure,* Shulevitz	A man travels afar to find that the treasure he seeks lies at home.
12	*How to Make an Apple Pie and See the World,* Priceman	A determined girl travels the world, collecting ingredients for her apple pie and making friends with whom to share it.
13	*Nate the Great,* Sharmat (series)	Child detective Nate tracks down clues for his strange friend Rosalind.
14	*Amelia Bedelia,* Parish (series)	Ditsy Amelia Bedelia's troubles with homophones provoke many misadventures and hilarity.
15	*Dandelion,* Freeman	When Dandelion reinvents himself for tea with Jennifer Giraffe, he is unrecognizable.

1st Grade

Conflict	Theme	Aids/Devices	Alternate Title	Week
Man vs Man, Man vs. Nature	Pacifism, individuality	Teacher Guide at CenterForLit website	*The Church Mouse,* Graham	1
Man vs. Nature, Man vs. Self	Bravery, love	Sensory Language, Repetition	*Blueberries for Sal ,* McCloskey	2
Man vs. Self, Man vs. Society	Foolishness, childishness, coming of age	Alliteration, imagery	*Waiting to Waltz ,* Rylant	3
Man vs. Nature, Man vs. Self	Bravery, determination, loyalty, integrity	*Ready Readers* at CenterForLit website	*The Wing Shop ,* Woodruff	4
Man vs. Man	Friendship, shrewdness, coming of age	Auido Lecture at CenterForLit website	*The Fool of the World and the Flying Ship,* Ransome	5
Man vs. Man	Respect for elders, the results of foolishness	Rhyme	*Jumanji,* Van Allsburg	6
Man vs. Nature	Kindness remembered, friendship	Alliteration, Anthropomorphism	*Tops and Bottoms,* Stevens	7
Man vs. Nature	Provision and care	Rhyme	*Ish,* Reynolds	8
Man vs. Nature, Man vs. Self	Growing up, self-control, hope	Imagery, Metaphor, Simile	*The Crock of Gold ,* Stobbs	9
Man vs. Nature (space), Man vs. Man	Family affection	*Ready Readers* at CenterForLit website	*Days of the Blackbird,* de Paola	10
Man vs. Self	Perseverance, faith, obedience, generosity	Irony	*Madeline's Rescue,* Bemelmans	11
Man vs. Man, Man vs. Nature	Determination, ingenuity, geography	Alliteration	*The Judge ,* Zemach	12
varies with story	varies with story	Alliteration	*Duffy and the Devil ,* Zemach	13
Man vs. Self, Man vs. Man	Miscommunication, patience	Circumstantial Irony	*How the Ostrich Got Its Long Neck,* Aardema	14
Man vs. Self, Man vs. Man	Pretense vs. reality	Rhyme, symbolism, double entendre	*The Crane Wife ,* Bodkin	15

Week	Title	Plot
16	*The Gardener,* Stewart	Lydia Grace Finch leaves her family to live with her uncle during the Great Depression.
17	*Horton Hears a Who,* Seuss	Horton the elephant hears tiny voices on a floating dust mote and struggles to protect the tiny lives they represent in spite of his skeptical, scoffing neighbors.
18	*Miss Rumphius,* Cooney	Miss Rumphius travels the world looking for a way to make it more beautiful.
19	*Sam, Bangs and Moonshine,* Ness	A motherless girl entertains and comforts herself with fantastical imaginings until her fictions endanger her neighbor friend, Thomas, and her beloved pet, Bangs.
20	*The Biggest Bear,* Ward	When little Johnny's pet bear cub grows to become a neghborhood nuisance, he must make a man's decision.
21	*Make Way for Ducklings,* McCloskey	Mr. and Mrs. Mallard search for a safe place to hatch and raise their ducklings.
22	*Chrysanthemum,* Henkes	Chrysanthemum loves her unusual name until her peers tease her about it.
23	*Wilfrid Gordon McDonald Partridge,* Fox	Wilfrid, a small boy who lives next to a retirement home, searches for his friend Miss Nancy's lost memory.
24	*Henry and Mudge,* Rylant (series)	Henry loves his big dog, Mudge, with whom he has myriad adventures.
25	*Leo the Late Bloomer,* Kraus	Little Leo is a bit behind the other tigers his age, but his mother knows he'll grow into himself.
26	*Little Bear,* Minarik (series)	Follow Little Bear as he engages in imaginative play and friendships.
27	*Snap!,* Vaughan	While little Joey's mother sleeps, he plays games with his friends, but Slytooth is no friend at all.
28	*The Biggest House in the World,* Lionni	A foolish snail, determined to have the largest, most opulent home in the world, grows a shell too large and consequently is unable to move when food supplies run short.
29	*The Great Gracie Chase,* Rylant	When painters, disturbing the peace of her home, accidentally leave a door ajar, Gracie the dog escapes and leads a growing group of friends and neighbors on a great chase.
30	*Snowflake Bentley,* Azarian	A biography of Willam Bentley, a student of nature, who learns photography in order to better study and share the natural artistry of snowflakes with the world.

1ˢᵗ Grade

Conflict	Theme	Aids/Devices	Alternate Title	Week
Man vs. Society, Man vs. Self, Man vs. Man	Bloom where you are planted. The value of beauty. Grace.	Teacher Guide at CenterForLit website	*The Empty Pot*, Demi	16
Man vs. Society	Sanctity of life, Faith, Persecution	Rhyme	*The Stranger*, VanAllsburg	17
Man vs. Self, Man vs. Nature	Altruism	Flashback	*The Cat In the Hat*, Seuss	18
Man vs. Self, Man vs. Nature	Discontentment, reality vs. imagination	Imagery	*The Velveteen Rabbit*, Williams	19
Man vs. Nature, Man vs. Self, Man vs. Man	Meaning of manhood, courage; Coming of Age	Understatement	*Caps For Sale*, Slobodkina	20
Man vs. Nature	Domestic harmony, man's stewardship of nature	Anthropomorphism	*Love You Forever*, Munsch	21
Man vs. Society, Man vs. Self	Insecurity, Peer pressure, Identity	Imagery, double entendre, alliteration	*Bedtime For Frances*, Hoban	22
Man vs. Nature, Man vs. Self	Friendship across generations, the faith of a child, the human experience.	Symbolism	*Sammy the Seal*, Hoff	23
varies with story	varies with story	Repetition	*The Polar Express*, VanAllsburg	24
Man vs. Self, Man vs. Society	individualism, patience	Anthropomorphism	*Mike Mulligan and His Steam Shovel*, Burton	25
varies with story	Maternal love, friendship, imagination	Repetition	*Paper John*, Small	26
Man vs. Man, Man vs. Self	Deception, Cleverness/Ingenuity	Onomatopoeia, alliteration	*The True Story of Pocahontas*, Penner	27
Man vs. Self	Modest thrift, humility, forethought	Frame	*The Boy Who Fooled the Giant*, Kitt	28
Man vs. Nature	He who is chased will run!	Repetition	*Baby Brains*, James	29
Man vs. Nature	Perseverance, diligence, patience, vision	Simile, Metaphor, Biography	*Sir Kevin of Devon*, Holl	30

1st Grade

Week	Title	Plot
31	*Petunia,* Duvoisin	Petunia is a silly goose determined to convince the other barnyard animals that she can read.
32	*Five Chinese Brothers,* Wiese	When one Chinese brother is convicted for the death of a child, his four brothers use their singular gifts to deliver him from execution.
33	*The Spider & the Fly,* DiTerlizzi	A spider lures a fly through flattery in this retelling of the beloved cautionary tale.
34	*Fishing in the Air,* Creech	A father and son take a fishing trip and catch more than they expect.
35	*Bread and Jam for Frances,* Hoban	Frances, a picky eater, learns to love variety when her mother feeds her desire for a bread and a jam diet.
36	*It Could Always Be Worse,* Zemach	When a Jewish man bemoans the smallness of his house to his Rabbi, he is given a sure antidote for discontentment.

Conflict	Theme	Aids/Devices	Alternate Title	Week
Man vs. Self	Dangers of pride and pretense	Alliteration	*Journey Cake, Ho!*, Sawyer	31
Man vs. Man, Man vs. Society	Good vs. Evil, Honor, Loyalty, Brotherly Love	Circumstantial Irony	*The Selfish Giant*, Wilde	32
Man vs. Man, Man vs. Self	Dangers of flattery, pride	Rhyme, Narrative Poem	*The Glorious Flight*, Provensen	33
Man vs. Nature	Ephemeral nature of time, importance of family traditions	*Ready Readers* at CenterForLit website	*A Baby Sister for Frances,* Hoban	34
Man vs. Man, Man vs. Self	Willfulness, being careful what you wish for	Irony	*The Tale of Jemima Puddleduck,* Potter	35
Man vs. Man, Man vs. Self	Perspective and Attitude are everything	Irony, sarcasm	*Many Moons*, Thurber	36

2nd Grade

Week	Title	Plot
Weeks 1-5	*Mouse Soup* , Lobel	Shrewd Mouse invents stories to entertain Weasel and escape becoming his dinner.
Weeks 6-9	*Frog and Toad series,* Lobel	Frog and Toad seem unlikely companions because of their disparate social classes, but remain loving friends despite these obstacles.
Weeks 10-13	*Mercy Watson* series, DiCamillo	Mercy Watson, a pet pig with a penchant for buttered toast, finds herself in a series of escapades with her loveable owners.
Weeks 14-18	*My Father's Dragon* , Gannet	The narrator relates the story of his clever father, Elmer Elevator, who journeys to the land of Tangerina to free a dragon who's been enslaved by the other islanders.
Weeks 19-23	*The Bears On Hemlock Mountain* , Dagliesh	When a young boy travels over the mountain on an errand for his mother, he discovers that there **are** bears on Hemlock Mountain.
Weeks 24-27	*The Minstrel In the Tower,* Skurzynski	Alice and Roger, siblings, travel by foot to find their estranged uncle and bring him to their sick mother's aid; a lute adorned with an eagle is the only proof of their identities.
Weeks 28-30	*Next Spring An Oriole* , Whelan	Ten year old Libby and her family travel by covered wagon to the property her father purchased in the unpeopled state of Michigan.
Weeks 31-36	*The Matchlock Gun* , Edmonds	Young Edward, his mother and his little sister must protect themselves from unfriendly indians while father is away fighting with the militia.

Conflict	Theme	Aids/Devices	Alternate Title	Week
Man vs. Man	Mouse proves the value of reading and thinking in this humorous tale; shrewdness.	Story frame	*The 100 Dresses*, Estes	Weeks 1-5
Varies from episode to episode	Friendship	Narrative repetition	*The Whipping Boy*, Fleischman	Weeks 6-9
Varies from episode to episode	Varies from episode to episode	Onomatopoeia, imagery, simile, rhyme, repetition	*The Reluctant Dragon*, Grahame	Weeks 10-13
Man vs. Nature, Man vs. Society	Forethought, kindness, friendship, compassion, loyalty	Alliteration	*Benjamin West and His Cat, Grimalkin,* Henry	Weeks 14-18
Man vs. Nature, Man vs. Self	Courage and responsibility, actions and consequences	Foreshadowing, imagery, repetition	*Stuart Little,* White	Weeks 19-23
Man vs. Man, Man vs. Nature	The enduring love of family	Symbolism	*A Bear Called Paddington*, Bond (Since this book is episodic, chapters can be studied in isolation.)	Weeks 24-27
Man vs. Nature	Hope, determination, vision, perseverance, hardship	Assonance, alliteration, symbolism	Nate the Great, Sharmat	Weeks 28-30
Man vs. Man, Man vs Self	Courage, obedience, coming of age	Foreshadowing	*Billy Blaze adventures,*	Weeks 31-36

3rd Grade

Week	Title	Plot
1	*Dr. De Soto*, Steig	Dr. De Soto, a mouse and the town dentist, must employ not only his expertise but also his wits when he treats a wily and hungry fox who has a tooth ache.
2	*Winnie the Pooh, "The House at Pooh Corner - In Which Eeyore Finds the Wolery and Owl Moves Into It"*, Milne	When Owl loses his home to a wind storm, the other residents of the 100 acre wood help him relocate.
3	*Chicken Sunday,* Polacco	Some children work to buy their beloved Miss Eula the Easter hat she's always wanted.
4	*Horton Hears A Who*, Seuss	Horton's keen ears hear better than most and make him alone responsible for protecting the wee people of Who-ville from annihilation.
5-8	*The Cricket In Times Square*, Selden	Chester the cricket and Mario the newsboy learn the self-sacrificial nature of real friendship as they endeavor to care for one another.
9-12	*The Mouse and the Motorcycle,* Cleary	Ralph, a mouse who lives in a roadside inn with his family, befriends and saves the life of a young boy, who rewards him with a gift of a toy motorcycle.
13-16	*Little House On the Prairie*, Wilder	Laura and her family, Ma, Pa, Mary, and Baby Carrie, stake a claim on the Western prairie, carving a home from the wilderness, but find they must abandon their efforts when the government sets the land aside for the indians.
17-20	*Ramona the Pest*, Cleary	Eight year old Ramona Quimby proves difficult for her family and classmates as she struggles with her own willfulness in an effort to grow up.
21-24	*Misty of Chincoteague*, Henry	Paul and Maureen Bibee work hard to earn money to buy the famous Phantom and her colt at the yearly pony auction on Chincoteague Island.
25-28	*The Hundred Dresses*, Estes	Maggie, horrified when her silent complicity to classroom bigotry forces classmate Wanda from town, must live with her guilt and the unanswered question of Wanda's fate.
29-32	*The Cabin Faced West,* Fritz	Ten year old Ann Hamilton, a dissatisfied and lonely pioneer girl in Pennsylvania, learns the satisfaction hard labor brings and becomes personally invested in her family's pioneer vision.
33-36	*Charlotte's Web*, White	When Fern's petted piglet Wilbur moves to the barn, his loneliness and fears are abated by his friendship with Charlotte, a sagacious grey barn spider.

Conflict	Theme	Aids/Devices	Alternate Title	Week
Man vs. Man	Courage, ethics, consequences. The triumph of good vs. evil. "He who lays a trap for another, his own feet will find it."	Anthropomorphism, Irony, Foreshadowing	*Ben and Me,* Lawson	1
Man vs. Nature Man vs. Man Man vs. Self	Self-sacrificial love and friendship	Personification	*Pippi Longstocking* , Lindgren	2
Man vs. Man	Honesty, character, kindness, love. Patience in the face of wrongful accusation	Frame	*Encyclopedia Brown* , Lobel	3
Man vs. Man Man vs. Society	Self-Sacrifice, Mob violence, the Value of life ("A person's a person no matter how small!")	Rhyme	*The Boxcar Children* , Warner	4
Man vs. Nature Man vs. Self	The nature of friendship; the importance of freedom	*Ready Readers* at CenterForLit website	*Henry and Ribsy* , Cleary	5-8
Man vs. Nature Man vs. Man Man vs. Self	Personal responsibility, courage, friendship	Alliteration, assonance, onomatopoeia, anthropomorphism	*Homer Price* , McCloskey	9-12
Man vs. Nature Man vs. Man Man vs. Society	Survival, Homesteading, Perseverance, Cooperation, Ingenuity, Community	Alliteration, assonance, imagery	*The Moffats* , Estes	13-16
Man vs. Man Man vs. Self	Childish rebellion, Humor, Irony	Homonym	*Kenny and the Dragon* , DiTerlizzi	17-20
Man vs. Nature Man vs. Self Man vs. Man	Stewardship/Dominion Mandate; Selfishness vs Selflessness; Sacrificial love; Coming of Age	*Ready Readers* at CenterForLit website	*The Great Brain* , Fitzgerald	21-24
Man vs. Man Man vs. Self Man vs. Society	Racism, Guilt, Complicity, Consequences, It is better to suffer a wrong than to do one.	Alliteration	*The Mouse of Amherst* , Spires (together with the poetry of Emily Dickinson)	25-28
Man vs. Nature Man vs. Self	Suffering and hardship produce character and fruitfulness; westward expansion	Symbolism, assonance, alliteration	*Stuart Little* , White	29-32
Man vs. Nature Man vs. Self Man vs. Man	Self- Sacrificial love and friendship: "Greater love has no man than this, that he would lay down his life for a friend."	Anthropomorphism	*A Little Princess* , Burnett	33-36

4th Grade

Week	Title	Plot
1	*Lentil,* McCloskey	For Lentil, a young boy whose singing voice is a bit below par, playing the harmonica is just the thing; his town thinks so too when he saves the day with his talent.
2	*Bedtime For Frances,* Hoban	Frances, a badger, hates bedtime and does her best to delay it.
3	*Apples To Oregon,* Hopkinson	Delicious and her daddy are determined to move their family and their orchard to the temperate state of Oregon.
4	*Elbert's Bad Word,* Wood	When Elbert tries out a bad word he has heard an adult utter, it turns into a monster that terrorizes him.
5-8	*Mr. Popper's Penguins,* Atwater	When Mr. Popper, a poor housepainter with big dreams, receives penguins by post from an Arctic explorer, he devises a plan by which to provide for both them and his family.
9-12	*Wind In the Willows,* Grahame	Fickle Mr. Toad of Toad Hall becomes entranced by the faddish new motorcar; his friends endeavor to recall him to his senses and restore to him his dignity and place in the community.
13-16	*The Thirteen Clocks,* Thurber	A cold Duke keeps his warm niece, Princess Saralinda, for himself, driving away suitors through cruelty and abuse until Prince Xingu, with the help of the Golux, rescues her.
17-20	*Charlie and the Chocolate Factory,* Dahl	When Charlie Bucket discovers a golden ticket in his Wonka Bar, he embarks on an adventure that tests his character and reveals his personal integrity.
21-24	*Adam of the Road,* Gray	Adam loses his minstrel father while chasing the thieves who've stolen his beloved dog; he travels a year searching for both father and dog and earning his bread as a minstrel.
25-28	*Trumpet of the Swan,* White	Louis, a swan born mute, learns to communicate by means of a trumpet that his father steals from a local music store; with the trumpet, he earns enough money to repay his father's debt to the store owner.
29-32	*Snow Treasure,* McSwigan	The children of a town occupied by Nazis during WWII are given the important responsibility of smuggling the national treasure out of the country.
33-36	*Miracle On Maple Hill,* Sorenson	A young girl and her family return to her mother's childhood home on Maple Hill in search of rest and respite for their father, a recovered POW.

Conflict	Theme	Aids/Devices	Alternate Title	Week
Man vs. Self Man vs. Man	Cheerfulness, diligence, value of the individual	Onomatopoeia	*How the Grinch Stole Christmas* , Seuss	1
Man vs. Man Man vs. Self	Obedience, consequences	Rhyme, onomatopoeia	*Roxaboxen,* Cohen	2
Man vs. Nature Man vs. Society Man vs. Self	Determination, Cooperation, Vision, Westward Expansion, the Pioneer Spirit, Industry	*Ready Readers* at CenterForLit website	*Stellaluna,* Canon	3
Man vs. Self	Importance of character and integrity in speech	Personification	*A Birthday for Frances,* Hoban	4
Man vs. Nature	Ingenuity, Singlemindedness, Vision	Alliteration	*The Jungle Books* , Kipling	5-8
Man vs. Man Man vs. Society Man vs. Self	City vs. Country, Industrialization, Urbanization, Value of community, Social Hierarchy, True Friendship	Classics Club DVD at CenterforLit website	*Owls In the Family* , Mowat	9-12
Man vs. Man	Good vs. Evil, the nature of faith, selfishness	Irony	*Detectives In Togas* , Winterbourne	13-16
Man vs. Society Man vs. Self Man vs. Man	Value of personal integrity, Honesty, Deception	Rhyme, symbolism	*The Penderwicks,* Birdsall	17-20
Man vs. Man	Perseverance, Patience, the Sin Nature of man, Coming of Age	Poetic devices common to lyric poetry	*The Secret Garden* , Burnett	21-24
Man vs. Man Man vs. Self Man vs. Nature	Character qualities such as determination, integrity, commitment, ethics; remuneration; fatherly love	*Ready Readers* at CenterForLit website	*Swiss Family Robinson* , Wyss	25-28
Man vs. Society Man vs. Man Man vs. Self	Bravery, patriotism, leadership, self-control	Personification, allusion	*The Whipping Boy* , Fleischman	29-32
Man vs. Society Man vs. Self Man vs. Nature	Regeneration/Renewal, Value of Community, Coming of Age/Growing Up	*Ready Readers* at CenterForLit website	*Five Children and It* , Nesbit	33-36

5th Grade

Week	Title	Plot
1	*The Little House*, Burton	Urban expansion leaves a little country house suddenly surrounded by skyscrapers.
2	*Why Mosquitoes Buzz In People's Ears,* Aardema	In this African fable, a mosquito's foolishness touches off an unexpected, tragic chain of events.
3	*Chrysanthemum,* Henkes	Chrysanthemum overcomes peer teasing and learns to love her name.
4	*TheBee Tree*, Polacco	A girl, tired of struggling with books, goes with her grandfather on a bee tree hunt and learns to savor the sweet rewards of hard won success.
5-8	*A Door In the Wall*, DeAngeli	Robin, a young nobleman's son, is struck with paralysis and abandoned by his household; a monk nurses him to health and teaches him self-discipline, industry, and respect for others.
9-12	*Otto of the Silver Hand,* Pyle	A bitter feud between two medieval barons causes great suffering for their children.
13-16	Shakespeare Intro using Lamb's Tales, "Macbeth" and the original play *Macbeth,* Shakespeare	When noble Macbeth, tempted by evil spirits, murders his kinsman and king, he finds he may keep his ill-gotten crown only through further bloodshed.
17-20	*The Penderwicks*, Birdsall	A motherless trio of sisters and their family dog befriend a rich but lonely boy one summer while vacationing in the rental cottage on his parents' estate.
21-24	*Straw Into Gold,* Schmidt	Drawing on the timeless fairytale of *Rumplestiltskin,* this story provides a reason for the little man's seemingly capricious act.
25-28	*The Chronicles of Narnia*, Lewis	The Pevensie children stumble into another land by way of an enchanted wardrobe and come to know not only themselves, but also the Lord of the land, Aslan, and the nature of love.
29-32	*The Indian in theCupboard*, Banks	Omri discovers that the old cupboard his brother gives him for his birthday has magical abilities to turn toys into living creatures, but he's unprepared for the implications of this lifegiving power.
33-36	*The Tale of Desperaux*, DiCamillo	Desperaux, the only mouse to survive from his litter, perpetually disappoints both his French mother and the rest of the mouse community with his nonconformity; still, he survives this rejection and fulfills his purpose providentially.

Conflict	Theme	Aids/Devices	Alternate Title	Week
Man vs. Society	Urbanization, City vs. Country	Personification	*The Reluctant Dragon,* Grahame	1
Man vs. Man Man vs. Himself	Actions have consequences.	Onomatopoeia	*The Apple and the Arrow ,* Buff	2
Man vs. Man Man vs. Himself	Self-confidence, Fear of Man, Peer problems, envy/jealousy	Pun	*King Arthur The Sword in the Stone ,* Talbott	3
Man vs. Nature Man vs. Himself	Sweetness of hard won success, perseverance, rewards of diligence	Alliteration, Dialect, Rhyme, Symbolism	*When I Was Young in the Mountains ,* Rylant	4
Man vs. God Man vs. Self Man vs. Nature Man vs. Society	Goodness and character are born through suffering. Providence. Grace	*Ready Readers* at CenterForLit website	*From the Mixed Up Files of Mrs. Basil E. Frankweiler ,* Konigsburg	5-8
Man vs. Man Man vs. Self	Effects of bitterness both personally and generationally, Forgiveness.	Symbolism	*The Dancing Bear, Dickinson*	9-12
Man vs. Self Man vs. Society Man vs. Man Man vs. Fate	Sin Nature (Fatal Flaw), Deceitfulness of the human heart, Dangers of selfish ambition	Poetic devices, blank verse, pun, double entendre	*The Invention of Hugo Cabret ,* Selznick	13-16
Man vs. Man Man vs. Self Man vs. Society	Family love, friendship, loyalty	Onomatopoeia, personification, allusion, flashback	*On the Wings of Heroes ,* Richard Peck	17-20
Man vs. Man Man vs. Society Man vs. Self Man vs. Providence	Selfless Love, Comparison and discussion of strength and weakness, Providence, Appearance vs. Reality	Frame, Imagery, Foreshadowing, Sensory Language	*Soup,* Robert Newton Peck	21-24
Man vs. Man Man vs. Self Man vs. Society Man vs. God	Sin Nature of Man, Sacrificial Love and Substitutionary Atonement, Redemption, the effects of Envy, Betrayal	Frame, Symbolism, Anthropomorphism	*Voyage of the Dawn Treader ,* Lewis	25-28
Man vs. Self Man vs. Man Man vs. God	The nature of human life and responsibility.	Foreshadowing	*The Silver Chair ,* Lewis	29-32
Man vs. Society Man vs. Self Man vs. Man	Betrayal ("perfidy"), providence, social pressure/prejudice,individuality, courtly love, and honor.	Symbolism, Alliteration, Imagery	*Beauty,* McKinley	33-36

Week	Title	Plot
1	*The Gardener*, Stewart	Lydia Grace must leave her family and live with her uncle in the city during the depression; her cheerful countenance and graciousness make her a blessing to everyone around her.
2	*Paul Revere's Ride*, Longfellow	The great American Poet Laureate tells the story of Paul Revere's famous ride to alert the Minutemen of the British soldiers' approach on the eve of the battle of Lexington & Concord in 1775.
3	*Crossing Bok Chitto*, Tingle	The friendship between an African American slave child and a Native American child facilitates a slave escape.
4	*The Library*, Stewart	A bookworm is overrun by the books she loves.
5-8	*Tuck Everlasting*, Babbitt	A young girl befriends the Tuck family, who have accidentally discovered the fountain of youth. She must decide whether to live a natural life herself and how to help them keep their secret from those who would exploit it.
9-12	*Julius Caesar*, Shakespeare	Brutus, Cassius and the other conspirators plot and perform the assassination of Julius Caesar. They then fight with the Triumvirate for control of Rome, only to find that the ambitious spirit for which they killed Caesar dwells in their own hearts as well.
13-16	*The Adventures of Tom Sawyer*, Twain	Mischievous Tom "plays, fights and hides" his way through childhood in small town Missouri, searching for hidden treasure and narrowly escaping the clutches of the evil Injun Joe.
17-20	*Little Women*, Alcott	Four sisters (Amy, Jo, Meg and Beth) face the challenges of growing up.
21-24	*The Scarlet Pimpernel*, Orczy	British gentleman Percy Blakeney pretends to be a worthless fop to hide his true identity as the daring leader of a shrewd plot to smuggle French aristocrats into England to escape the Reign of Terror.
25-28	*At the Back of the North Wind*, MacDonald	A sickly boy journeys with the mythical North Wind to faraway lands and learns of her trustworthiness, faithfulness and love.
29-32	*I Am David*, Holm	Young David, who has lived his whole life separated from his parents in a Nazi concentration camp, escapes with the help of a prison guard and must walk north across Europe to find freedom and happiness.
33-36	*Treasure Island*, Stevenson	Jim Hawkins, whose family is deeply in debt, discovers a pirate's treasure map and embarks on a dangerous journey to find the treasure, encountering honest men and ruffians in equal measure along the way.

Daily/Weekly Model

Conflict	Theme	Aids/Devices	Alternate Title	Week
Man vs. Society Man vs. Man Man vs. Self	Bloom where you are planted A cheerful heart does good like a medicine	Teacher Guide at CenterForLit website	*The Friend*, Stewart	1
Man v. Man Man v. Society	Patriotism Liberty	*Teaching the Classics* basic seminar	*The Old Woman Who Named Things*, Rylant	2
Man v. Man Man v. Society	Friendship across racial boundaries; the incongruity of slavery	Teacher Guide at CenterForLit website	*Grandfather's Journey*, Say	3
Man v. Self	The joys of sharing Philanthropy	Rhyme	*Song and Dance Man*, Ackerman	4
Man v. Nature Man v. Man Man v. Self	The story explores the natural order of things and the consequences of upsetting this order.	Symbolism, Imagery	*Anne of Green Gables*, Montgomery	5-8
Man v. Man Man v. Self Man v. Society	The wickedness of the human heart The law of sowing and reaping Tyranny Ambition Frailty	*Ready Readers* at CenterForLit website	*Mrs. Frisbee & the Rats of NIMH*, O'Brien	9-12
Man v. Man Man v. Nature	A reminiscence of boyhood The wonder of childhood Human nature	Irony, Allusion	*Black Ships Before Troy*, Sutcliffe	13-16
Man v. Nature Man v. Man Man v. Self	Faithfulness, thrift, patience generosity and love. Change, though painful, is not an evil.	Symbolism, imagery, allegory, allusion	*Little Britches*, Moody	17-20
Man v. Man Man v. Society	Appearances vs. Reality Heroism Loyalty and Trust Love	Circumstantial Irony	*Caddie Woodlawn*, Brink	21-24
Man v. God Man v. Man	This allegory explores the problem of pain and the nature of death while depicting goodness, kindness and charity.	*Ready Readers* at CenterForLit website	*A Girl of the Limberlost*, Porter	25-28
Man v. Man Man v. Society	Sacrificial love Faith, Hope and Trust Determination	Symbolism	*The Witch of Blackbird Pond*, Speare	29-32
Man v. Man Man v. Self	Coming of Age Shrewdness/Resourcefulness Honesty Mercy Friendship	*Ready Readers* at CenterForLit website	*The Pushcart War*, Merrill	33-36

7th Grade

Week	Title	Plot
1	*The Keeping Quilt,* Polacco	A Russian immigrant makes an heirloom quilt for her daughter out of the rag clothing of family members she's left behind.
2	*All Those Secrets of the World,* Yolen	Janie gets a lesson in perspective and learns to believe in the continued existence of people who are absent when her father goes away to war.
3	*Amos & Boris,* Steig	When the mouse Amos's ship capsizes, he is rescued by the whale Boris; years later, Amos returns the favor unexpectedly.
4	*A Bargain for Frances,* Hoban	When Frances's friend Thelma takes advantage of her, Frances finds a way to get even.
5-8	*The Bronze Bow*, Speare	Daniel bar-Jamin, a rugged runaway who has cast his lot with the zealots, is recalled to responsibility by his grandmother's death. He must wrestle with his hatred for the Romans who occupy Israel and his growing love for his people.
9-12	*The Odyssey,* Homer	Odysseus, who has struggled 10 years in the Trojan war and been delayed from homecoming another 10 years for offending the gods, finally regains his home.
13-16	*Huckleberry Finn,* Twain	Vagabond Huck and runaway slave Jim try to escape society by floating down the Mississippi River on a raft.
17-20	Short Story Unit: *To Build a Fire,* London; *The Telltale Heart,* Poe; *The Most Dangerous Game,* Connell	In *To Build a Fire,* a solitary man struggles to survive in the icy Yukon; in *The Telltale Heart,* a deranged murderer boasts of his shrewd deception; in *The Most Dangerous Game,* a cruel hunter uses shipwreck survivors as prey on his private island.
21-24	*Great Expectations*, Dickens	When the impoverished orphan Pip discovers that he has come into an inheritance from a mysterious benefactor, he distances himself from his humble friends and family to better himself and earn the love of the wealthy and beautiful Estella.
25-28	*Watership Down*, Adams	When Hazel's brother, Fiver, predicts doom for their warren, Hazel leads a group of their friends into the wilderness to establish a new home on Watership Down.
29-32	*Johnny Tremain*, Forbes	Johnny, proud apprentice to a Boston silversmith, experiences apparent tragic setbacks which providentally place him in strategic places to witness the momentous events of the Revolutionary War and spur him towards personal maturity.
33-36	*The Hiding Place*, Ten Boom	The true story of Corrie Ten Boom and her family, who are caught sheltering Jews from the Nazis in WWII Holland. They are arrested and sent to a concentration camp, where they must struggle to survive.

Conflict	Theme	Aids/Devices	*Alternate Title*	Week
Man v. Nature	The value of family heritage	Symbolism	*The Fool of the World and the Flying Ship,* Ransome	1
Man v. Society	Patience Hope Faith Belief	Tone	*Anatole,* Titus	2
Man v. Nature	Friendship Kindness Faithfulness & Loyalty	Descriptive language, Irony	*Casey At the Bat,* retold by Polacco	3
Man v. Man Man v. Self	Deception Shrewdness Friendship Coming of Age	Audio Lecture at CenterForLit website	*Thunder Cake,* Polacco	4
Man v. Society Man v. Self Man v. God	Bitterness & its Effects The nature of forgiveness Sacrificial love Redemption	*Ready Readers* at CenterForLit website	*The Devil's Arithmetic,* Yolen	5-8
Man v. gods Man v. Man	The importance of marriage and family Faithfulness Patriotism and loyalty Justice	Epic Simile	*The Wanderings of Odysseus,* Sutcliffe (a re-telling of The Odyssey for young readers)	9-12
Man v. Sociey Man v. Man Man v. Self	Freedom & Slavery Character & Integrity Racism Pride vs. Humility Social Conventions	Classics Club DVD at CenterForLit website	*Henry V,* Shakespeare	13-16
Man vs. Nature Man vs. Himself Man vs. Man	All three stories are commentaries on human nature from various perspectives	Worldview seminar at CenterForLit website	*A Connecticut Yankee In King Arthur's Court,* Twain	17-20
Man v. Self Man v. Man Man vs. Society	Redemptive Love Pride vs. Humility Appearance vs. Reality Fear of Man; Bitterness Coming of Age; Friendship	Symbolism, imagery, allegory, foreshadowing	*Kidnapped,* Stevenson	21-24
Man v. Society Man v. Nature [Man v. Man/Self]	A study of human Totalitarianism Tyranny vs. Freedom Leadership Faith, Fear, Bravery	Anthropomorphism, Foreshadowing	*Here There Be Dragons,* Owen	25-28
Man vs. Man Man vs. Himself Man vs. God Man vs. Society	Effects of Pride Providental love Sanctification Courage and Self-Sacrifice Freedom	Metaphor, symbolism, personification, imagery	*A Gathering of Days,* Blos	29-32
Man v. Society Man v. Self Man v. God Man v. Man	Redemptive Love God's grace & sovereignty Forgiveness Bitterness The sinful nature of man	Foreshadowing, irony	*The 100 Cupboards,* Wilson	33-36

8th Grade

Week	Title	Plot
1	*I Have an Olive Tree,* Bunting	7 year old Greek immigrant Sophie wants a skateboard for her birthday; instead, Grandpa gives her an olive tree in their homeland.
2	*The Biggest Bear,* Ward	A young boy must rid the neighborhood of his beloved pet bear, who has become a nuisance.
3	*Thank You, Mr. Falker,* Polacco	A 5th grade student who struggles with dyslexia overcomes her problem with the help of a kind teacher.
4	*Letting Swift River Go,* Yolen	Visiting the inundated Swift River Valley which once was her home, Sally Jane makes peace with her drowned past.
5-8	*The Iliad,* Homer	Greek warrior and demi-god Achilles, embittered by King Agamemnon's ill treatment, refuses to reconcile and withdraws from the battle between the Greeks and the Trojans.
9-12	*The Yearling,* Rawlings	Jody must give up his childhood and embrace the responsibilities of a man when his pet fawn grows up to menace the family farm.
13-16	*A Tale of Two Cities,* Dickens	Exiled aristocrat Charles Darnay returns to France during the Reign of Terror; without the aid of family friend Sydney Carton, he will be executed, leaving his family desolate.
17-20	*Across Five Aprils,* Hunt	As the American Civil War divides his family, young Jethro must journey with the nation from youth to maturity.
21-24	*King Arthur & the Book of the Three Worthies,* Pyle	In three tales, Pyle explores the chivalric code and its virtues with the wider aim of discussing human nature.
25-28	*The Hobbit,* Tolkien	Homebody Bilbo Baggins is petitioned by the wizard Gandalf to accompany a group of dwarves on a mission to burgle stolen treasure from the evil dragon Smaug.
29-32	*Call it Courage,* Sperry	A young boy must master his fear of the sea in this coming-of-age adventure.
33-36	*Carry On, Mr. Bowditch,* Latham	Nathaniel Bowditch is a math whiz and longs to be a Harvard man;. his apprenticeship forces him to "sail by ash breeze," gaining him character, achievement and acclaim.

Conflict	Theme	Aids/Devices	Alternate Title	Week
Man vs. Man	Heritage Maturity	Symbolism	*Eleanor,* Cooney	1
Man v. Nature Man v. Self Man v. Society	Manhood/Masculinity What is courage? Self-denial What is strength?	Pun, parody, irony, understatement	*Mirette On the High Wire,* McCulley	2
Man v. Man Man v. Self	Faithfulness Belief Enduring Love	Allusion, metaphor	*The Tale of Custard the Dragon,* Nash	3
Man v. Society Man v. Nature Man v. Self	The nature of time Bitterness & forgiveness Link between acceptance & peace	*Ready Readers* at CenterForLit website	*Angelo,* Macaulay	4
Man v. Man Man v. Self Man v. gods	Bitterness & its consequences Honor Pride Loyalty & Friendship	Epic Simile, *In Medias Res*	*Black Ships Before Troy,* Sutcliffe (a re-telling of the Iliad for children)	5-8
Man v. Nature Man v. Man Man v. Self	Coming of Age Childhood v. Manhood	Classics Club DVD at CenterForLit website	*A Connecticut Yankee in King Arthur's Court,* Twain	9-12
Man v. Society Man v. Man Man v. Self	Sacrificial Love Bitterness & Revenge Faithfulness & Devotion Tyranny & Liberty	Teacher Guide at CenterForLit website	*A Wrinkle in Time,* L'Engle	13-16
Man v. Society Man v. Man	Social pressure to conform Persecution Forgiveness Coming of Age	Dialect, irony, foreshadowing, symbolism	*The Witch of Blackbird Pond,* Speare	17-20
Man v. Self Man v. Man	Good vs. Evil The sinful nature of man Repentance **Honor** Vanity/Pride vs. Humility	Symbolism	*Cheaper by the Dozen,* Gilbraith	21-24
Man v. Self Man v. Man Man v. Society	Greed vs. Contentment Faithfulness, Selflessness Appearances v. Realities Strength coming from Weakness Good v. Evil	*Ready Readers* at CenterForLit website	*The House of 60 Fathers,* Meindert de Jong	25-28
Man v. Self Man v. Nature	The Nature of Courage Coming of Age Superstition	Personification	*A Girl of the Limberlost,* Porter	29-32
Man v. Self Man v. God Man v. Nature	Perseverance/Patience Providence The nature of obstacles Puritan work ethic Faithfulness in little things	*Ready Readers* at CenterForLit website	*Banner in the Sky,* Ullman	33-36

9th Grade

Week	Title	Plot
1	*Fishing In the Air*, Creech	A boy and his father go on a fishing trip and catch more than they expect.
2	*Owl Moon*, Yolen	A child experiences a family rite of passage when he goes owling with his father.
3	*All the Places to Love,* MacLachlan	A boy remembers all the places he's come to love and the people with whom they're associated, promising to share them with his new baby sister.
4	*St. George and the Dragon,* Hyman & Hodges	Based on Edmund Spenser's *The Fairie Queene*, this is the story of Brave Sir George who, sought out by Princess Una, fights a dragon to win her hand in marriage.
5-8	*The Aeneid*, Virgil	Aeneas flees a burning Troy and journeys with other refugees to establish a new homeland on the coast of Italy.
9-12	*Sir Gawain and the Green Knight,* retold by Tolkien	Gawain, a knight of the renowned Round Table, finds his character and integrity tested when he accepts a challenge from a mysterious knight.
13-16	*Don Quixote (abridged),* Cervantes	A Spanish landowner, who spends his idle hours reading chivalric romances, fancies himself a knight. Engaging a squire with promises of a dukedom, he travels the countryside jousting at windmills and generally acting the fool in this classic satire.
17-20	*Romeo and Juliet,* Shakespeare	Impetuous teen lovers from feuding families forsake their parents' authority when they marry secretly; disaster ensues.
21-24	*Frankenstein,* Shelley	Scientific genius Victor Frankenstein seeks immortality by creating life. His creature does not meet expectations. The disastrous consequences that follow force us to face questions about the nature of man, God and Nature.
25-28	*The Strange Case of Dr. Jekyll and Mr. Hyde,* Stevenson	A narrator discovers that the respectable doctor he has long called his friend is also the mysterious menace who has committed a string of heinous crimes in late 19th century London.
29-32	*The Chosen*, Potok	An unlikely friendship between two boys -- one an orthodox and the other a liberal Jew -- exposes cultural differences and leads to greater self-knowledge on the part of both friends.
33-36	*The Fellowship of the Ring*, Tolkien	Young Frodo Baggins accepts a quest to destroy the Ring, whose power could destroy Middle Earth. Frodo is aided by a motley group of elves, dwarves and men - and by the mysterious wizard Gandalf.

Conflict	Theme	Aids/Devices	Alternate Title	Week
Man vs. Nature Man vs. Self	Family Heritage, the Nature of Time, Memory	*Ready Readers* at CenterForLit website	*Don Quixote,* Williams	1
Man vs. Nature Man vs. Self	Self-control, Patience, Coming of Age	Imagery, Simile, Metaphor	*Sir Gawain and the Green Knight,* Morpurgo	2
Man vs. Nature	Generational heritage, the value of the land, mortality	*Ready Readers* at CenterForLit website	*Albert,* Napoli	3
Man vs. Nature Man vs. Self	Courage Courtly Love Chivalry	Allusion, type, symbolism	*Wee Gillis ,* Leaf	4
Man v. Society Man v. Man Man v. the gods	Providence Patriotism - superiority of national to personal vision	Epic simile, alliteration, personification, allegory, irony	*The Prince and the Pauper ,* Twain	5-8
Man v. Man Man v. Self	Importance of honor Importance of chastity Importance of self-control	Convention, metaphor, oxymoron, simile, symbolism	*The Black Arrow ,* Stevenson	9-12
Man v. Self Man v. Society	Ridiculousness of chivalric romance Virtue, Morality, Goodness Realism vs. Idealism	The predecessor of the novel as a literary genre	*The Three Musketeers,* Dumas	13-16
Man v. Man Man v. God	Consequences of bitterness, and rashness Consequences of rebellion Dangers of deception Star crossed love	Poetic devices: blank verse, pun, irony, etc.	*Merchant of Venice ,* Shakespeare	17-20
Man v. Nature Man v. God Man v. Man	What is a human being? Creature/Creator distinction	Flashback	*Good Morning, Miss Dove,* Patton	21-24
Man v. Man Man v. Self Man v. God Man v. Nature	Human Nature Original Sin Role of the Conscience Pride & Ambition	Foreshadowing	*The Black Falcon ,* Sperry	25-28
Man v. Society Man v. Self	Coming of Age Faith vs. Religion Fathers and Sons	Symbolism, metaphor	*1984,* Orwell	29-32
Man v. Man Man v. Self Good vs. Evil	Seduction of ambition Strength in weakness Fellowship Sacrificial Love; Mercy Corruption of sin	Symbolism, foreshadowing	*The Two Towers ,* Tolkien or *The Return of the King ,* Tolkien	33-36

Week	Title	Plot
1	*Beowulf,* picture storybook	Beowulf the Geat, hero of his people, voyages to the land of king Hrothgar, to whom he owes a family debt. There he delivers Hrothgar's people from the monster scourge Grendel.
2	*Canterbury Tales,* retold by Barbara Cohen	An introduction to the famous tales of Geoffrey Chaucer, this book includes short re-tellings of the Nun's Priest's Tale, the Pardoner's Tale, the Wife of Bath's Tale and the Franklin's Tale.
3	*Canterbury Tales,* retold by Barbara Cohen	An introduction to the famous tales of Geoffrey Chaucer, this book includes short re-tellings of the Nun's Priest's Tale, the Pardoner's Tale, the Wife of Bath's Tale and the Franklin's Tale.
4	*The Clown of God,* DePaola	An orphan boy discovers his talent for juggling and makes a place for himself in society. When old age eventually robs him of it, he finds he still has place with God.
5-8	*Beowulf*	Beowulf the Geat, hero of his people, voyages to the land of king Hrothgar, to whom he owes a family debt. There he delivers Hrothgar's people from the monster scourge Grendel.
9-12	*City of God,* Augustine (selections)	Genre: Philosophical Treatise (non-fiction). Augustine contends with accusations that Christians were responsible for the fall of Rome and exposes by reasonable argument the philosophical and spiritual folly of worshiping the gods.
13-16	*Divine Comedy: The Inferno,* Dante	Genre: Epic Poetry. In his middle age, the narrator, aided by the beautiful Beatrice and guided by the wise poet Virgil, travels through hell to understand the nature, breadth and consequences of sin.
17-20	*Canterbury Tales,* Chaucer (selections: General Prologue, Nun's Priest's Tale, Pardoner's Tale, Knight's Tale)	A diverse group of 14th century English men and women meet on a pilgrimage to the cathedral at Canterbury. They decide to pass time along the journey with a storytelling contest.
21-24	*The Taming of the Shrew,* Shakespeare	Genre: Play. Sharp-tongued Katerina meets her match when overbearing and shrewd Petrucchio weds and woos her.
25-28	*The Great Divorce,* Lewis	A day trip to the outer regions of Heaven gives inhabitants of Hell a once-in-a-lifetime opportunity: to experience paradise and its "Solid People" and choose their own citizenship.
29-32	*The Count of Monte Cristo,* Dumas	Unjustly imprisoned, the main character spends years plotting and then executing revenge upon those who ruined his life.
33-36	*The Hound of the Baskervilles,* Doyle	Sherlock Holmes disillusions spiritualists and uncovers a very material plot to kill Sir Henry Baskerville.

Conflict	Theme	Aids/Devices	Alternate Title	Week
Man v. Animal/Monster, Man vs. Fate	Honor Good triumphs over evil The strength of virtue Fate	Kennings	*The Sign Painter,* Say	1
Conflicts vary, but all include Man v. Self, Man v. God	Human Nature Dangers of Pride, Greed Forgiving Debts	Allusion, irony, parody, allegory	*Chanticleer and the Fox*, Cooney	2
Coflicts vary, but all include Man v. Self, Man v. God	Human Nature Dangers of Pride, Greed Forgiving Debts	Allusion, irony, parody, allegory	*Sir Gawain and the Loathly Lady*, Hastings	3
Man v. Society Man v. Self Man v. Nature Man v. God	Value of human life The holiness of all callings The joy of service	*Ready Readers* at CenterForLit website	*Yellow and Pink,* Steig	4
Man v. Animal/Monster, Man vs. Fate	Honor Good triumphs over evil The strength of virtue	Kennings	*Dream of the Rood* or Caedmon's *Hymn*	5-8
Christianity v. polytheism Man v. Society	Irrationality of pluralism Virtue Civic benefits of virtue (historical document)	Overstatement, apology, sarcasm	*Confessions,* Augustine (selections)	9-12
Man v. Self Man v. Man Man v. God	Fallen human nature Retributive Justice	Meter, epic simile, allegory, symbolism, allusion	*The Banquet*, Dante or *The Secret*, Petrarch	13-16
Every type of conflict is fully explored in this masterpiece	Human nature and its foibles The dangers of various character flaws Good triumphs over evil	Understatement, allegory, fable, irony	*Everyman*, Anonymous Medieval Drama	17-20
Man v. Man Man v. Self Man vs. Society	Marriage and male headship Love Authority and Submission Femininity Appearances vs. Reality	Blank verse, irony, pun	Alternate Shakespearean Comedies: *Midsummer Night's Dream or The Tempest*	21-24
Man v. Self Man v. God	Bitterness, salvation Vanity, vice Deception Pride	Teacher Guide at CenterForLit website	*Till We Have Faces*, Lewis or *The Screwtape Letters*, Lewis	25-28
Man v. Man Man v. Self	Injustice Revenge Bitterness and Hatred Deception	Symbolism, allusion	*The Three Musketeers,* Dumas	29-32
Man vs. Man Man vs. Self	Materialism Murder Superstition Rationalism	Red herring	The *Father Brown Mysteries*, GK Chesterton	33-36

Week	Title	Plot
1	*The Dangerous Journey* , Oliver Hunkin	An illustrated *Pilgrim's Progres* s for children, this allegory follows a man, Christian, on his journey through life's perils to heaven's gates.
2	*The Giving Tree,* Silverstein	A chronicle of the lifelong friendship between a boy and a tree.
3	*Wilfrid Gordon Macdonald Partridge,* Fox	Wilfrid, a small boy, helps Miss Nancy, his elderly frend, find her memory.
4	*The Spider and the Fly* , DiTerlizzi	A flattering spider entices a gullible fly into his parlor.
5-8	*Paradise Lost* , Milton	The fallen angel, Lucifer, seeks revenge upon the Creator God by conducting a sneak attack on His newest creation, man.
9-12	*Hamlet,* Shakespeare	The noble prince of Denmark decides to avenge his father's murder, but struggles to make good on his pledge.
13-16	*Pilgrim's Progress* , Bunyan	Christian, tormented by spiritual anguish, follows his guide Evangelist on a journey from the City of Destruction to Mount Zion, the holy city
17-20	*Gulliver's Travels* , Swift (selections)	Gullible Gulliver's travels take him to curious kingdoms, each of which provides opportunities for him to see his own pride and foolishness.
21-24	*Faust,* Goethe (Book I)	Dr. Faust, unfulfilled by the wealth of knowledge he's gathered, sells his soul to the devil to obtain all his heart's desire.
25-28	*Bleak House* , Dickens	Orphan Esther Summerson seeks friendship and belonging among a family of Chancery suitors, while the noble Lady Dedlock struggles to protect a horrible secret.
29-32	*Wuthering Heights* , Bronte	A traveler uncovers the secret past of a wild and violent landowner, Heathcliff, and his one time beloved Kathy.
33-36	*Pride and Prejudice* , Austen	Elizabeth Bennet, jaded by Mr. Darcy's arrogance towards her, forms a prejudice against him that only desperate circumstances and valorous actions can overcome.

Conflict	Theme	Aids/Devices	Alternate Title	Week
Man vs. Man Man vs. Self Man vs. the World	Redemption, Grace, perseverance of the saints, the struggle against sin and the world	Allegory	*Three Names*, MacLachlan	1
Man vs. Man	Self-sacrificial love	Personification	*Always Room For One More*, Leodhas	2
Man vs. Nature Man vs. Self	The universal human experience The nature of friendship	*Ready Readers* at CenterForLit website	*The Tale of Meshka the Kvetch*, Chapman	3
Man vs. Man Man vs. Self	Dangers of flattery/pride	Anthropomorphism	*Song of the Swallows*, Politi	4
Creature vs. Creator, Man vs. man	The Fall of Man Origins of Sin	Epic Simile, Epic devices	*Lycidas,* Milton	5-8
Man vs. Himself Man vs. Fate Man vs. Man	Human frailty The Tragic Hero Sanity vs. Insanity Revenge	Classics Club DVD at CenterForLit website	*Henry V,* Shakespeare	9-12
Man vs. Himself Man vs. Society Man vs. Man	Good vs. Evil Spiritual growth Salvation	Allegory	*The Importance of Being Earnest*, Wilde	13-16
Man vs. Man Man vs. Himself Man vs. Society	The value of self-knowledge Humility Creaturehood of man	Allegory	*A Modest Proposal*, Swift	17-20
Man vs. God Man vs. Man Man vs. Self	Destructiveness of self-love Danger of Subverting Nature Perversity of Sin	Tragic Hero, irony, types, epic devices	*Alice in Wonderland*, Carroll	21-24
Man vs. Society Man vs. Man	Justice	Simile, personification, imagery	*David Copperfield*, Dickens	25-28
Man vs. Man Man vs. Society	Perverse love/Selfish love The nature of passion Revenge/Bitterness/Betrayal Manipulation Social Prejudice	Gothic Romance, symbolism, imagery	*The Dubliners*, Joyce	29-32
Man vs. Man Man vs. Society	Social Mores and Prejudices Honor/Virtue in both men and women	Irony (also makes use of satire)	*Jane Eyre, Bronte*	33-36

12th Grade

Week	Title	Plot
1	*Emily,* Bedard	A curious child chronicles her relationship with her introverted neighbor, the poet Emily Dickinson.
2	*Henry David's House,* Schnur	Henry David Thoreau builds a cabin and spends a year communing with nature. A picture book look at *Walden.*
3	*The Man Who Walked Between the Towers,* Gerstein	True life narrative of the French tightrope artist who walked a wire strung between the historic twin towers.
4	*The Wall,* Sis	A Czechoslovakian boy grows up in a communist state.
5-8	*Last of the Mohicans,* Cooper	English soliders, American scouts and Mohican and Huron warriors engage in battle, intrigue and romance during the 18th century French and Indian War.
9-12	*Uncle Tom's Cabin,* Stowe	In spite of persecution, Tom, a Southern American black slave, continually proves himself heroic by selflessly sacrificing himself for others.
13-16	*The Scarlet Letter,* Hawthorne	American Puritan Hester Prynn and her illegitimate daughter Pearl suffer public shame for her adultery while the unnamed father remains hidden, bearing his guilt in secret.
17-20	*The Red Badge of Courage,* Crane	Young and naïve Henry joins the Union Army with visions of valour and heroism, but finds such valor impossible in a world without universal truth and meaning.
21-24	Hemingway Unit: *The Old Man and the Sea,* "Today Is Friday," "A Clean, Well-Lighted Place"	An old Cuban fisherman, Santiago, fallen on hard luck, hooks the largest fish of his career only to have it consumed by sharks before he can bring it to shore.
25-28	Flannery O'Connor short stories: *Revelation, A Good Man Is Hard to Find, The Lame Shall Enter First*	Upstanding, self-righteous Southerners encounter violent calamities that force them (and the reader) to consider the nature of man and the state of their souls.
29-32	*A Day In the Life of Ivan Denisovitch,* Solzhenitsyn	A Russian man struggles to retain his humanity in the face of the abuses of a Soviet concentration camp.
33-36	*To Kill A Mockingbird,* Lee	Two children, Scout and Jem, become both witnesses and victims to social bigotry and racism when their father, a court appointed lawyer, defends an innocent black man accused of raping a white woman.

Conflict	Theme	Aids/Devices	Alternate Title	Week
Man vs. Society	Reclusiveness/Shyness Quiet Joy Friendship	Rhythm, metaphor, alliteration, simile, personification	*My Uncle Emily*, Yolen	1
Man vs. Society Man vs. Nature	Naturalism Pantheism Darwinism Self-Sufficiency, Simplicity	Alliteration, understatement	*The Other Side*, Woodson	2
Man vs. Society Man vs Nature	Dreams/Visions Daring	Alliteration	*So Few Of Me*, Reynolds	3
Man vs. Society Man vs. Man Man vs. Nature	Freedom vs. Tyranny, the triumph of the human spirit	Imagery	*The Three Golden Keys*, Sis	4
Man vs. Man Man vs. Society Man vs. Nature Man vs. Fate	The "Noble Savage" Heroism Loyalty Revenge	Types, symbolism, imagery	*Heart of Darkness*, Conrad	5-8
Man vs. Man Man vs. Society	Self-Sacrificial Love Horrors Definition of Manhood Slavery vs. Freedom	Symbolism, monologue, allusion	*Rabble In Arms*, Roberts	9-12
Man vs. Society Man vs. Self Man vs. God Man vs. Man	Consequences of adultery (sin) Effects of unconfessed sin/guilty Effects of bitterness Revenge Slavery vs. Freedom	Symbolism	*The Last of the Mohicans*, Cooper	13-16
Man vs. Nature Man vs. Man Man vs. Self Man vs. Society	Mechanization of man Brutality of war The importance of empathy Determinism	Symbolism, imagery, metaphor, simile	*The Open Boat*, Crane	17-20
Man vs. Nature Man vs. Himself Man vs. Fate	Grace under pressure Empathy Disinterestedness of nature Courage in the face of a meaningless world	Symbolism, allusion	*The Pearl*, Steinbeck or *Of Mice and Men*, Steinbeck	21-24
Man vs. God Man vs. Man Man vs. Society Man vs. Himself	Human depravity Divine Grace Prejudice Self-righteousness	Irony	Edgar Allan Poe Shorts: *The Tell-Tale Heart, The Pit and the Pendulum, The Cask of Amontillado*	25-28
Man vs. Man Man vs. Society Man vs. Self	The indomitable human spirit Freedom vs. Tyranny Atrocity of Communism	Symbolism	*The Death of Ivan Ilyich*, Tolstoy	29-32
Man vs. Man Man vs. Society Man vs. Himself	Lost innocence Coming of Age Self-Sacrifical Love Racial Prejudice Source of Virtue/Honor	Symbolism, allusion, simile, metaphor	*The Call of the Wild*, London	33-36

Chapter 2

The Monthly Model

The Monthly Model

The Monthly Model is designed for home schools, homeschool co-ops, book clubs, or any group conducting monthly one to two-hour classes. For these groups, literature is a high priority.

Kindergarten and First Grade:

In a monthly class that is 1 hour in length, read the story aloud to the students, then teach and discuss the major elements of fiction in turn, as follows:

Month 1 – Setting and Characters

Month 2 – Conflict and Plot

Month 3 – Themes and Literary Devices.

Months 4-9 - In the remaining months, utilize the plot chart and the method presented in *Teaching the Classics* basic seminar to lead the kids in reading and plotting stories on the plot chart, always aiming in the end for a discussion of basic, eternal themes. Crafts and activities may be developed to support the story presentation if time allows.

Second Grade:

Second graders will spend the first monthly meeting learning to identify story elements and use the plot chart to arrive at a discussion of theme. Teachers will read aloud from the picture books listed for Class 1, discussing the structural elements of story as presented in *Teaching the Classics*. The remainder of the year, teachers will take up one story from the second grade list per class meeting, treating it in its entirety. In this way, the students will have read and discussed a total of 2 story books and 8 books at grade level by the end of the academic year. All reading from the main reading list will be done with parents outside of class before the day of discussion. Classes will focus on comprehension and analysis rather than phonics skills. Again, enrichment activities may be scheduled for each meeting (art projects, etc.) if time allows.

A sample schedule follows:

Month 1 – Read 2 picture story books and introduce story elements and plot chart in a 1-2 hr. class.

Month 2 – Discuss book 1 in its entirety in a 1-2 hour class.

Month 3 – Discuss book 2 in its entirety in a 1-2 hour class.

Month 4 – Discuss book 3 in its entirety in a 1-2 hour class.

Month 5 – Discuss book 4 in its entirety in a 1-2 hour class.

Month 6 – Discuss book 5 in its entirety in a 1-2 hour class.

Month 7 – Discuss book 6 in its entirety in a 1-2 hour class.

Month 8 – Discuss book 7 in its entirety in a 1-2 hour class.

Month 9 – Discuss book 8 in its entirety in a 1-2 hour class.

Third through Twelfth Grades:

All of the reading assignments are completed in advance of the class meetings with the exception of the initial class, during which the discussion leader will read and discuss two picture books and present a model for analysis that will guide discussions for the remainder of the year. Each two hour class meeting that follows will treat one novel in its entirety. A sample format follows:

Month 1 – Read aloud and discuss the children's books suggested at the beginning of your grade level reading list. Take time to teach the elements of story as presented in the *Teaching the Classics* basic seminar. A sample schedule for the first meeting is below:

- Read picture book #1 and introduce the story elements of character, setting, conflict and plot.
- Plot the story on a plot chart. Introduce the 5th element of story, theme. Identify it.
- Using picture book #2, fully plot the story on a plot chart, identifying elements of setting, character, conflict and any themes as they fit into the plot structure and events of the story.

Your method for presenting these elements will depend upon how much training in literature your students have previously had. For younger students or students new to the study of literature, use this time to arm them with a literary vocabulary and a familiarity with the structural elements of literature. Older students may already be familiar with these things; use their first class to talk about the usefulness of structure in revealing a story's themes. Spend time identifying literary devices, figurative language, etc. Acclimate them to the Socratic questioning method and the use of the story chart. The picture books we have chosen are deeply thematic, written for adults as well as children. This unit is often the students' favorite class of the year.

Whenever possible, we have chosen picture books for each year that either anticipate or resonate with books on the grade level reading list. For example, Ward's *The Biggest Bear* shares many themes with Rawlings' *The Yearling*. Cohen's illustrated *Canterbury Tales* makes a great introduction to Chaucer's original.

Month 2 – Student should come to class having read the first title on the main reading list. Make sure students all read the same edition and bring their copies to class. Discuss the story in one 2-hour discussion, leading the kids through the elements of story structure to arrive at a discussion of thematic ideas. Begin class with background information about the author and the period in which the story was written. Include any contextual details that might help them to understand the work more fully. Utilize the plot chart to encourage students to think carefully about the story's structure. Who is the main character? What is the main conflict? How is this resolved? Pay special attention to your placement of the climax as this will inform your understanding of the author's themes.

Conflicts, conflict resolution, and themes are all intimately connected. Sometimes, there exists more than one possibility for the placement of the climax. Make students defend their choice with details from the text. How does this event resolve the greater story conflicts? What might the author be trying to say by way of this climax? Utilize the Socratic List (located in the Appendix to the *Teaching the Classics* basic seminar) to stimulate discussion. Be sure to note any literary devices the author employed. Here's a summary of the elements you should address:

Identification of:

- Context
- Literary Devices
- Setting
- Characters
- Conflict
- Plot/Structural Elements
- Themes/Motifs

Months 3 through 9 – Repeat this type of discussion with a new title every month to cover a total of 2 picture books and 8 novels in a nine month (36 week) academic year. As the students grow accustomed to the discussion, you can deepen your questioning by adding some elements of comparative or "worldview" analysis. For example, discuss how the stories answer the following questions:

- What's a good life?
- What good is life?
- What's a good death?
- What good is death?
- What's a good love?
- What good is love? [1]
- How do the author's answers to these questions compare with those of other works you've studied?
- How do his answers compare with your own ideas?

The Monthly Model adequately allows for the treatment of books at a basic level, with time for analysis, appreciation of stylistic devices and author's voice, and a book's place in the Western Canon.

---

[1] Thanks to Michael Bauman, Ph.D., our professor at Hillsdale College, for teaching us to ask these questions back in 1989.

Kindergarten

Class	Title	Plot
1	*The Bee Tree, Polacco*	A reluctant reader learns the sweetness of hard won success when her grandfather takes her on a bee hunt.
2	*The Tale of Peter Rabbit*, Potter	Peter disobeys his mother's order and sneaks into Mr. McGregor's garden, losing his new clothes and catching a terrible cold.
3	*Rainbow Fish*, Pfister	The lovely, rainbow-colored fish wins friends by sharing.
4	*Apples to Oregon*, Hopkinson	Daddy and Delicious embark on a journey from Iowa to Oregon with a "nursery" wagon full of fruit trees and hearts full of hope.
5	*Red Riding Hood*, Grimm	A little girl disobeys her mother by straying from the path on the way to visit her grandma.
6	*Harriet, You'll Drive Me Wild,* Fox	Little Harriet doesn't mean to trouble her mother any more than her mother means to lose her temper, but when Harriet's childish mistakes snowball, both find themselves in need of forgiveness.
7	*Cinderella*, Rackham	An orphaned girl, abused by her stepmother and stepsisters, wins the heart of a handsome prince with the help of her fairy-godmother.
8	*Peter and the Wolf*, Prokofiev	When Peter goes beyond the garden gate, he is stalked by a ravenous wolf.
9	*The Keeping Quilt*, Polacco	An immigrant family preserves its heritage and memories in a special keepsake: a quilt that becomes a family heirloom.

Conflict	Theme	Aids/Devices	Alternate Title	Class
Man vs. Nature, Man vs. Self	Rewards of patience and perseverance, the sweetness of success	Alliteration, Dialect, Symbolism	*Why Mosquitoes Buzz in People's Ears* , Aardema	1
Man vs. Man, Man vs. Nature	Consequences of disobedience	*Teaching the Classics* basic seminar	*The Tale of Benjamin Bunny* , Potter	2
Man vs. Self	Self-sacrifice, sharing	Circumstantial irony	*Just Plain Fancy* , Polacco	3
Man vs. Nature	Determination, perseverance, cooperation, vision	*Ready Readers* at CenterForLit website	*King Bidgood's In the Bathtub* ,Wood	4
Man vs. Nature, Man vs. Man	Consequences of disobedience	Foreshadowing	*Beauty and the Beast* , Grimm	5
Man vs. Man, Man vs. Self	Self-control, patience, repentance forgiveness and reconciliation	*Ready Readers* at CenterForLit website	*Alexander and the Terrible, Horrible, No Good, Very Bad Day,* Viorst	6
Man vs. Man	Rewards of goodness, good vs. evil	Irony	*Thy Friend, Obadiah* , Turkle	7
Man vs. Nature	Man's dominion over nature	Anthropomorphism	*The Whispering Rabbit,* Brown	8
Man vs. Nature	The preservation of heritage and family in the face of time's passage	Symbolism	*Thank You, Mr. Falker* , Polacco	9

1st Grade

Class	Title	Plot
1	*The Story of Ferdinand,* Leaf	Unlike the other bulls, Ferdinand refuses to fight in the bullfights in Madrid, preferring peaceful contemplation in his meadow.
2	*Brave Irene,* Steig	When her seamstress mother is taken ill, young Irene braves a snowstorm to deliver a gown commissioned by the duchess.
3	*A Bargain for Frances,* Hoban	Frances, swindled by her friend Thelma, gets even.
4	*Owl Moon,* Yolen	A father and child go owling in this coming of age classic.
5	*The Gardener,* Stewart	Lydia Grace Finch leaves her family to live with her uncle during the Great Depression.
6	*Horton Hears a Who,* Seuss	Horton the elephant hears tiny voices on a floating dust mote and struggles to protect the tiny lives they represent in spite of his skeptical, scoffing neighbors.
7	*Miss Rumphius,* Cooney	Miss Rumphius travels the world looking for a way to make it more beautiful.
8	*The Biggest Bear,* Ward	When little Johnny's pet bear cub grows to become a neghborhood nuisance, he must make a man's decision.
9	*Chrysanthemum,* Henkes	Chrysanthemum loves her unusual name until her peers tease her about it.

Conflict	Theme	Aids/Devices	Alternate Title	Class
Man vs Man, Man vs. Nature	Pacifism, individuality	Teacher Guide at CenterForLit website	*The Church Mouse,* Graham	1
Man vs. Nature, Man vs. Self	Bravery, determination, loyalty, integrity	*Ready Readers* at CenterForLit website	*The Wing Shop* , Woodruff	2
Man vs. Man	Friendship, shrewdness, coming of age	Auido Lecture at CenterForLit website	*The Fool of the World and the Flying Ship,* Ransome	3
Man vs. Nature, Man vs. Self	Growing up, self-control, hope	Imagery, Metaphor, Simile	*The Crock of Gold* , Stobbs	4
Man vs. Society, Man vs. Self, Man vs. Man	Bloom where you are planted. The value of beauty. Grace.	Teacher Guide at CenterForLit website	*The Empty Pot* , Demi	5
Man vs. Society	Sanctity of life, Faith, Persecution	Rhyme	*The Stranger* , VanAllsburg	6
Man vs. Self, Man vs. Nature	Altruism	Flashback	*The Cat In the Hat* , Seuss	7
Man vs. Nature, Man vs. Self, Man vs. Man	Meaning of manhood, courage; Coming of Age	Understatement	*Caps For Sale* , Slobodkina	8
Man vs. Society, Man vs. Self	Insecurity, Peer pressure, Identity	Imagery, double entendre, alliteration	*Bedtime For Frances* , Hoban	9

Class	Title	Plot
1	*Amos and Boris,* Steig	The story of an unlikely friendship between a mouse and a whale reminiscient of Aesop's fable of the mouse and the lion.
1	*Corduroy,* Freeman	A small stuffed bear finds a home.
2	*Mouse Soup* , Lobel	Shrewd Mouse invents stories to entertain Weasel and escape becoming his dinner.
3	*Frog and Toad series,* Lobel	Frog and Toad seem unlikely companions because of their disparate social classes, but remain loving friends despite these obstacles.
4	*Mercy Watson* series, DiCamillo	Mercy Watson, a pet pig with a penchant for buttered toast, finds herself in a series of escapades with her loveable owners.
5	*My Father's Dragon* , Gannet	The narrator relates the story of his clever father, Elmer Elevator, who journeys to the land of Tangerina to free a dragon who's been enslaved by the other islanders.
6	*The Bears On Hemlock Mountain* , Dagliesh	When a young boy travels over the mountain on an errand for his mother, he discovers that there **are** bears on Hemlock Mountain.
7	*The Minstrel In the Tower,* Skurzynski	Alice and Roger, siblings, travel by foot to find their estranged uncle and bring him to their sick mother's aid; a lute adorned with an eagle is the only proof of their identities.
8	*Next Spring An Oriole* , Whelan	Ten year old Libby and her family travel by covered wagon to the property her father purchased in the unpeopled state of Michigan.
9	*The Matchlock Gun* , Edmonds	Young Edward, his mother and his little sister must protect themselves from unfriendly indians while father is away fighting with the militia.

Conflict	Theme	Aids/Devices	Alternate Title	Class
Man vs. Nature	Kindness remembered, friendship	Alliteration, Anthropomorphism	*Tops and Bottoms*, Stevens	1
Man vs. Self	Love, friendship	Personification	*Norman, the Doorman*, Freeman	1
Man vs. Man	Mouse proves the value of reading and thinking in this humorous tale; shrewdness.	Story frame	*The 100 Dresses*, Estes	2
Varies from episode to episode	Friendship	Narrative repetition	*The Whipping Boy*, Fleischman	3
Varies from episode to episode	Varies from episode to episode	Onomatopoeia, imagery, simile, rhyme, repetition	*The Reluctant Dragon*, Grahame	4
Man vs. Nature, Man vs. Society	Forethought, kindness, friendship, compassion, loyalty	Alliteration	*Benjamin West and His Cat, Grimalkin,* Henry	5
Man vs. Nature, Man vs. Self	Courage and responsibility, actions and consequences	Foreshadowing, imagery, repetition	*Stuart Little,* White	6
Man vs. Man, Man vs. Nature	The enduring love of family	Symbolism	*A Bear Called Paddington*, Bond (Since this book is episodic, chapters can be studied in isolation.)	7
Man vs. Nature	Hope, determination, vision, perseverance, hardship	Assonance, alliteration, symbolism	Nate the Great, Sharmat	8
Man vs. Man, Man vs Self	Courage, obedience, coming of age	Foreshadowing	*Billy Blaze adventures,*	9

3rd Grade

Class	Title	Plot
1	*Winnie the Pooh, "The House at Pooh Corner - In Which Eeyore Finds the Wolery and Owl Moves Into It",* Milne	When Owl loses his home to a wind storm, the other residents of the 100 acre wood help him relocate.
1	*Horton Hears A Who ,* Seuss	Horton's keen ears hear better than most and make him alone responsible for protecting the wee people of Who-ville from annihilation.
2	*The Cricket In Times Square ,* Selden	Chester the cricket and Mario the newsboy learn the self-sacrificial nature of real friendship as they endeavor to care for one another.
3	*The Mouse and the Motorcycle,* Cleary	Ralph, a mouse who lives in a roadside inn with his family, befriends and saves the life of a young boy, who rewards him with a gift of a toy motorcycle.
4	*Little House On the Prairie ,* Wilder	Laura and her family, Ma, Pa, Mary, and Baby Carrie, stake a claim on the Western prairie, carving a home from the wilderness, but find they must abandon their efforts when the government sets the land aside for the indians.
5	*Ramona the Pest ,* Cleary	Eight year old Ramona Quimby proves difficult for her family and classmates as she struggles with her own willfulness in an effort to grow up.
6	*Misty of Chincoteague ,* Henry	Paul and Maureen Bibee work hard to earn money to buy the famous Phantom and her colt at the yearly pony auction on Chincoteague Island.
7	*The Hundred Dresses ,* Estes	Maggie, horrified when her silent complicity to classroom bigotry forces classmate Wanda from town, must live with her guilt and the unanswered question of Wanda's fate.
8	*The Cabin Faced West,* Fritz	Ten year old Ann Hamilton, a dissatisfied and lonely pioneer girl in Pennsylvania, learns the satisfaction hard labor brings and becomes personally invested in her family's pioneer vision.
9	*Charlotte's Web ,* White	When Fern's petted piglet Wilbur moves to the barn, his loneliness and fears are abated by his friendship with Charlotte, a sagacious grey barn spider.

Conflict	Theme	Aids/Devices	Alternate Title	Class
Man vs. Nature Man vs. Man Man vs. Self	Self-sacrificial love and friendship	Personification	*Pippi Longstocking*, Lindgren	1
Man vs. Man Man vs. Society	Self-Sacrifice, Mob violence, the Value of life ("A person's a person no matter how small!")	Rhyme	*The Boxcar Children*, Warner	1
Man vs. Nature Man vs. Self	The nature of friendship; the importance of freedom	*Ready Readers* at CenterForLit website	*Henry and Ribsy*, Cleary	2
Man vs. Nature Man vs. Man Man vs. Self	Personal responsibility, courage, friendship	Alliteration, assonance, onomatopoeia, anthropomorphism	*Homer Price*, McCloskey	3
Man vs. Nature Man vs. Man Man vs. Society	Survival, Homesteading, Perseverance, Cooperation, Ingenuity, Community	Alliteration, assonance, imagery	*The Moffats*, Estes	4
Man vs. Man Man vs. Self	Childish rebellion, Humor, Irony	Homonym	*Kenny and the Dragon*, DiTerlizzi	5
Man vs. Nature Man vs. Self Man vs. Man	Stewardship/Dominion Mandate; Selfishness vs Selflessness; Sacrificial love; Coming of Age	*Ready Readers* at CenterForLit website	*The Great Brain*, Fitzgerald	6
Man vs. Man Man vs. Self Man vs. Society	Racism, Guilt, Complicity, Consequences, It is better to suffer a wrong than to do one.	Alliteration	*The Mouse of Amherst*, Spires (together with the poetry of Emily Dickinson)	7
Man vs. Nature Man vs. Self	Suffering and hardship produce character and fruitfulness; westward expansion	Symbolism, assonance, alliteration	*Stuart Little*, White	8
Man vs. Nature Man vs. Self Man vs. Man	Self-Sacrificial love and friendship: "Greater love has no man than this, that he would lay down his life for a friend."	Anthropomorphism	*A Little Princess*, Burnett	9

4ᵗʰ Grade

Class	Title	Plot
1	*Bedtime For Frances,* Hoban	Frances, a badger, hates bedtime and does her best to delay it.
1	*Apples To Oregon,* Hopkinson	Delicious and her daddy are determined to move their family and their orchard to the temperate state of Oregon.
2	*Mr. Popper's Penguins* , Atwater	When Mr. Popper, a poor housepainter with big dreams, receives penguins by post from an Arctic explorer, he devises a plan by which to provide for both them and his family.
3	*Wind In the Willows,* Grahame	Fickle Mr. Toad of Toad Hall becomes entranced by the faddish new motorcar; his friends endeavor to recall him to his senses and restore to him his dignity and place in the community.
4	*The Thirteen Clocks,* Thurber	A cold Duke keeps his warm niece, Princess Saralinda, for himself, driving away suitors through cruelty and abuse until Prince Xingu, with the help of the Golux, rescues her.
5	*Charlie and the Chocolate Factory* , Dahl	When Charlie Bucket discovers a golden ticket in his Wonka Bar, he embarks on an adventure that tests his character and reveals his personal integrity.
6	*Adam of the Road* , Gray	Adam loses his minstrel father while chasing the thieves who've stolen his beloved dog; he travels a year searching for both father and dog and earning his bread as a minstrel.
7	*Trumpet of the Swan,* White	Louis, a swan born mute, learns to communicate by means of a trumpet that his father steals from a local music store; with the trumpet, he earns enough money to repay his father's debt to the store owner.
8	*Snow Treasure* , McSwigan	The children of a town occupied by Nazis during WWII are given the important responsibility of smuggling the national treasure out of the country.
9	*Miracle On Maple Hill* , Sorenson	A young girl and her family return to her mother's childhood home on Maple Hill in search of rest and respite for their father, a recovered POW.

4th Grade

Conflict	Theme	Aids/Devices	Alternate Title	Class
Man vs. Man Man vs. Self	Obedience, consequences	Rhyme, onomatopoeia	*Roxaboxen,* Cohen	1
Man vs. Nature Man vs. Society Man vs. Self	Determination, Cooperation, Vision, Westward Expansion, the Pioneer Spirit, Industry	*Ready Readers* at CenterForLit website	*Stellaluna,* Canon	1
Man vs. Nature	Ingenuity, Singlemindedness, Vision	Alliteration	*The Jungle Books*, Kipling	2
Man vs. Man Man vs. Society Man vs. Self	City vs. Country, Industrialization, Urbanization, Value of community, Social Hierarchy, True Friendship	Classics Club DVD at CenterforLit website	*Owls In the Family*, Mowat	3
Man vs. Man	Good vs. Evil, the nature of faith, selfishness	Irony	*Detectives In Togas*, Winterbourne	4
Man vs. Society Man vs. Self Man vs. Man	Value of personal integrity, Honesty, Deception	Rhyme, symbolism	*The Penderwicks,* Birdsall	5
Man vs. Man	Perseverance, Patience, the Sin Nature of man, Coming of Age	Poetic devices common to lyric poetry	*The Secret Garden*, Burnett	6
Man vs. Man Man vs. Self Man vs. Nature	Character qualities such as determination, integrity, commitment, ethics; remuneration; fatherly love	*Ready Readers* at CenterForLit website	*Swiss Family Robinson*, Wyss	7
Man vs. Society Man vs. Man Man vs. Self	Bravery, patriotism, leadership, self-control	Personification, allusion	*The Whipping Boy*, Fleischman	8
Man vs. Society Man vs. Self Man vs. Nature	Regeneration/Renewal, Value of Community, Coming of Age/Growing Up	*Ready Readers* at CenterForLit website	*Five Children and It*, Nesbit	9

Class	Title	Plot
1	*Why Mosquitoes Buzz In People's Ears,* Aardema	In this African fable, a mosquito's foolishness touches off an unexpected, tragic chain of events.
1	*Chrysanthemum,* Henkes	Chrysanthemum overcomes peer teasing and learns to love her name.
2	*A Door In the Wall,* DeAngeli	Robin, a young nobleman's son, is struck with paralysis and abandoned by his household; a monk nurses him to health and teaches him self-discipline, industry, and respect for others.
3	*Otto of the Silver Hand,* Pyle	A bitter feud between two medieval barons causes great suffering for their children.
4	Shakespeare Intro using Lamb's Tales, "Macbeth" and the original play *Macbeth,* Shakespeare	When noble Macbeth, tempted by evil spirits, murders his kinsman and king, he finds he may keep his ill-gotten crown only through further bloodshed.
5	*The Penderwicks,* Birdsall	A motherless trio of sisters and their family dog befriend a rich but lonely boy one summer while vacationing in the rental cottage on his parents' estate.
6	*Straw Into Gold,* Schmidt	Drawing on the timeless fairytale of *Rumplestiltskin,* this story provides a reason for the little man's seemingly capricious act.
7	*The Chronicles of Narnia,* Lewis	The Pevensie children stumble into another land by way of an enchanted wardrobe and come to know not only themselves, but also the Lord of the land, Aslan, and the nature of love.
8	*The Indian in theCupboard,* Banks	Omri discovers that the old cupboard his brother gives him for his birthday has magical abilities to turn toys into living creatures, but he's unprepared for the implications of this lifegiving power.
9	*The Tale of Desperaux,* DiCamillo	Desperaux, the only mouse to survive from his litter, perpetually disappoints both his French mother and the rest of the mouse community with his nonconformity; still, he survives this rejection and fulfills his purpose providentially.

Conflict	Theme	Aids/Devices	Alternate Title	Class
Man vs. Man Man vs. Himself	Actions have consequences.	Onomatopoeia	*The Apple and the Arrow*, Buff	1
Man vs. Man Man vs. Himself	Self-confidence, Fear of Man, Peer problems, envy/jealousy	Pun	*King Arthur The Sword in the Stone*, Talbott	1
Man vs. God Man vs. Self Man vs. Nature Man vs. Society	Goodness and character are born through suffering. Providence. Grace	*Ready Readers* at CenterForLit website	*From the Mixed Up Files of Mrs. Basil E. Frankweiler*, Konigsburg	2
Man vs. Man Man vs. Self	Effects of bitterness both personally and generationally, Forgiveness.	Symbolism	*The Dancing Bear*, Dickinson	3
Man vs. Self Man vs. Society Man vs. Man Man vs. Fate	Sin Nature (Fatal Flaw), Deceitfulness of the human heart, Dangers of selfish ambition	Poetic devices, blank verse, pun, double entendre	*The Invention of Hugo Cabret*, Selznick	4
Man vs. Man Man vs. Self Man vs. Society	Family love, friendship, loyalty	Onomatopoeia, personification, allusion, flashback	*On the Wings of Heroes*, Richard Peck	5
Man vs. Man Man vs. Society Man vs. Self Man vs. Providence	Selfless Love, Comparison and discussion of strength and weakness, Providence, Appearance vs. Reality	Frame, Imagery, Foreshadowing, Sensory Language	*Soup,* Robert Newton Peck	6
Man vs. Man Man vs. Self Man vs. Society Man vs. God	Sin Nature of Man, Sacrificial Love and Substitutionary Atonement, Redemption, the effects of Envy, Betrayal	Frame, Symbolism, Anthropomorphism	*Voyage of the Dawn Treader*, Lewis	7
Man vs. Self Man vs. Man Man vs. God	The nature of human life and responsibility.	Foreshadowing	*The Silver Chair*, Lewis	8
Man vs. Society Man vs. Self Man vs. Man	Betrayal ("perfidy"), providence, social pressure/prejudice, individuality, courtly love, and honor.	Symbolism, Alliteration, Imagery	*Beauty,* McKinley	9

6th Grade

Class	Title	Plot
1	*The Gardener*, Stewart	Lydia Grace must leave her family and live with her uncle in the city during the depression; her cheerful countenance and graciousness make her a blessing to everyone around her.
1	*Paul Revere's Ride,* Longfellow	The great American Poet Laureate tells the story of Paul Revere's famous ride to alert the Minutemen of the British soldiers' approach on the eve of the battle of Lexington & Concord in 1775.
2	*Tuck Everlasting,* Babbitt	A young girl befriends the Tuck family, who have accidentally discovered the fountain of youth. She must decide whether to live a natural life herself and how to help them keep their secret from those who would exploit it.
3	*Julius Caesar,* Shakespeare	Brutus, Cassius and the other conspirators plot and perform the assassination of Julius Caesar. They then fight with the Triumvirate for control of Rome, only to find that the ambitious spirit for which they killed Caesar dwells in their own hearts as well.
4	*The Adventures of Tom Sawyer,* Twain	Mischievous Tom "plays, fights and hides" his way through childhood in small town Missouri, searching for hidden treasure and narrowly escaping the clutches of the evil Injun Joe.
5	*Little Women,* Alcott	Four sisters (Amy, Jo, Meg and Beth) face the challenges of growing up.
6	*The Scarlet Pimpernel,* Orczy	British gentleman Percy Blakeney pretends to be a worthless fop to hide his true identity as the daring leader of a shrewd plot to smuggle French aristocrats into England to escape the Reign of Terror.
7	*At the Back of the North Wind,* MacDonald	A sickly boy journeys with the mythical North Wind to faraway lands and learns of her trustworthiness, faithfulness and love.
8	*I Am David,* Holm	Young David, who has lived his whole life separated from his parents in a Nazi concentration camp, escapes with the help of a prison guard and must walk north across Europe to find freedom and happiness.
9	*Treasure Island,* Stevenson	Jim Hawkins, whose family is deeply in debt, discovers a pirate's treasure map and embarks on a dangerous journey to find the treasure, encountering honest men and ruffians in equal measure along the way.

Conflict	Theme	Aids/Devices	Alternate Title	Class
Man vs. Society Man vs. Man Man vs. Self	Bloom where you are planted A cheerful heart does good like a medicine	Teacher Guide at CenterForLit website	*The Friend* , Stewart	1
Man v. Man Man v. Society	Patriotism Liberty	*Teaching the Classics* basic seminar	*The Old Woman Who Named Things* , Rylant	1
Man v. Nature Man v. Man Man v. Self	The story explores the natural order of things and the consequences of upsetting this order.	Symbolism, Imagery	*Anne of Green Gables,* Montgomery	2
Man v. Man Man v. Self Man v. Society	The wickedness of the human heart The law of sowing and reaping Tyranny Ambition Frailty	*Ready Readers* at CenterForLit website	*Mrs. Frisbee & the Rats of NIMH,* O'Brien	3
Man v. Man Man v. Nature	A reminiscence of boyhood The wonder of childhood Human nature	Irony, Allusion	*Black Ships Before Troy,* Sutcliffe	4
Man v. Nature Man v. Man Man v. Self	Faithfulness, thrift, patience generosity and love. Change, though painful, is not an evil.	Symbolism, imagery, allegory, allusion	*Little Britches,* Moody	5
Man v. Man Man v. Society	Appearances vs. Reality Heroism Loyalty and Trust Love	Circumstantial Irony	*Caddie Woodlawn,* Brink	6
Man v. God Man v. Man	This allegory explores the problem of pain and the nature of death while depicting goodness, kindness and charity.	*Ready Readers* at CenterForLit website	*A Girl of the Limberlost,* Porter	7
Man v. Man Man v. Society	Sacrificial love Faith, Hope and Trust Determination	Symbolism	*The Witch of Blackbird Pond,* Speare	8
Man v. Man Man v. Self	Coming of Age Shrewdness/Resourcefulness Honesty Mercy Friendship	*Ready Readers* at CenterForLit website	*The Pushcart War,* Merrill	9

7th Grade

Class	Title	Plot
1	*Amos & Boris,* Steig	When the mouse Amos's ship capsizes, he is rescued by the whale Boris; years later, Amos returns the favor unexpectedly.
1	*A Bargain for Frances,* Hoban	When Frances's friend Thelma takes advantage of her, Frances finds a way to get even.
2	*The Bronze Bow*, Speare	Daniel bar-Jamin, a rugged runaway who has cast his lot with the zealots, is recalled to responsibility by his grandmother's death. He must wrestle with his hatred for the Romans who occupy Israel and his growing love for his people.
3	*The Odyssey,* Homer	Odysseus, who has struggled 10 years in the Trojan war and been delayed from homecoming another 10 years for offending the gods, finally regains his home.
4	*Huckleberry Finn,* Twain	Vagabond Huck and runaway slave Jim try to escape society by floating down the Mississippi River on a raft.
5	Short Story Unit: *To Build a Fire,* London; *The Telltale Heart,* Poe; *The Most Dangerous Game,* Connell	In *To Build a Fire,* a solitary man struggles to survive in the icy Yukon; in *The Telltale Heart,* a deranged murderer boasts of his shrewd deception; in *The Most Dangerous Game,* a cruel hunter uses shipwreck survivors as prey on his private island.
6	*Great Expectations*, Dickens	When the impoverished orphan Pip discovers that he has come into an inheritance from a mysterious benefactor, he distances himself from his humble friends and family to better himself and earn the love of the wealthy and beautiful Estella.
7	*Watership Down*, Adams	When Hazel's brother, Fiver, predicts doom for their warren, Hazel leads a group of their friends into the wilderness to establish a new home on Watership Down.
8	*Johnny Tremain*, Forbes	Johnny, proud apprentice to a Boston silversmith, experiences apparent tragic setbacks which providentially place him in strategic places to witness the momentous events of the Revolutionary War and spur him towards personal maturity.
9	*The Hiding Place*, Ten Boom	The true story of Corrie Ten Boom and her family, who are caught sheltering Jews from the Nazis in WWII Holland. They are arrested and sent to a concentration camp, where they must struggle to survive.

7th Grade

Conflict	Theme	Aids/Devices	*Alternate Title*	Class
Man v. Nature	Friendship Kindness Faithfulness & Loyalty	Descriptive language, Irony	*Casey At the Bat,* retold by Polacco	1
Man v. Man Man v. Self	Deception Shrewdness Friendship Coming of Age	Audio Lecture at CenterForLit website	*Thunder Cake,* Polacco	1
Man v. Society Man v. Self Man v. God	Bitterness & its Effects The nature of forgiveness Sacrificial love Redemption	*Ready Readers* at CenterForLit website	*The Devil's Arithmetic,* Yolen	2
Man v. gods Man v. Man	The importance of marriage and family Faithfulness Patriotism and loyalty Justice	Epic Simile	*The Wanderings of Odysseus,* Sutcliffe (a re-telling of The Odyssey for young readers)	3
Man v. Sociey Man v. Man Man v. Self	Freedom & Slavery Character & Integrity Racism Pride vs. Humility Social Conventions	Classics Club DVD at CenterForLit website	*Henry V,* Shakespeare	4
Man vs. Nature Man vs. Himself Man vs. Man	All three stories are commentaries on human nature from various perspectives	Worldview seminar at CenterForLit website	*A Connecticut Yankee In King Arthur's Court,* Twain	5
Man v. Self Man v. Man Man vs. Society	Redemptive Love Pride vs. Humility Appearance vs. Reality Fear of Man; Bitterness Coming of Age; Friendship	Symbolism, imagery, allegory, foreshadowing	*Kidnapped,* Stevenson	6
Man v. Society Man v. Nature [Man v. Man/Self]	A study of human Totalitarianism Tyranny vs. Freedom Leadership Faith, Fear, Bravery	Anthropomorphism, Foreshadowing	*Here There Be Dragons,* Owen	7
Man vs. Man Man vs. Himself Man vs. God Man vs. Society	Effects of Pride Providential love Sanctification Courage and Self-Sacrifice Freedom	Metaphor, symbolism, personification, imagery	*A Gathering of Days,* Blos	8
Man v. Society Man v. Self Man v. God Man v. Man	Redemptive Love God's grace & sovereignty Forgiveness Bitterness The sinful nature of man	Foreshadowing, irony	*The 100 Cupboards,* Wilson	9

Class	Title	Plot
1	*The Biggest Bear,* Ward	A young boy must rid the neighborhood of his beloved pet bear, who has become a nuisance.
1	*Letting Swift River Go,* Yolen	Visiting the inundated Swift River Valley which once was her home, Sally Jane makes peace with her drowned past.
2	*The Iliad,* Homer	Greek warrior and demi-god Achilles, embittered by King Agamemnon's ill treatment, refuses to reconcile and withdraws from the battle between the Greeks and the Trojans.
3	*The Yearling,* Rawlings	Jody must give up his childhood and embrace the responsibilities of a man when his pet fawn grows up to menace the family farm.
4	*A Tale of Two Cities,* Dickens	Exiled aristocrat Charles Darnay returns to France during the Reign of Terror; without the aid of family friend Sydney Carton, he will be executed, leaving his family desolate.
5	*Across Five Aprils,* Hunt	As the American Civil War divides his family, young Jethro must journey with the nation from youth to maturity.
6	*King Arthur & the Book of the Three Worthies,* Pyle	In three tales, Pyle explores the chivalric code and its virtues with the wider aim of discussing human nature.
7	*The Hobbit,* Tolkien	Homebody Bilbo Baggins is petitioned by the wizard Gandalf to accompany a group of dwarves on a mission to burgle stolen treasure from the evil dragon Smaug.
8	*Call it Courage,* Sperry	A young boy must master his fear of the sea in this coming-of-age adventure.
9	*Carry On, Mr. Bowditch,* Latham	Nathaniel Bowditch is a math whiz and longs to be a Harvard man;. his apprenticeship forces him to "sail by ash breeze," gaining him character, achievement and acclaim.

Conflict	Theme	Aids/Devices	Alternate Title	Class
Man v. Nature Man v. Self Man v. Society	Manhood/Masculinity What is courage? Self-denial What is strength?	Pun, parody, irony, understatement	*Mirette On the High Wire*, McCulley	1
Man v. Society Man v. Nature Man v. Self	The nature of time Bitterness & forgiveness Link between acceptance & peace	*Ready Readers* at CenterForLit website	*Angelo,* Macaulay	1
Man v. Man Man v. Self Man v. gods	Bitterness & its consequences Honor Pride Loyalty & Friendship	Epic Simile, *In Medias Res*	*Black Ships Before Troy,* Sutcliffe (a re-telling of the Iliad for children)	2
Man v. Nature Man v. Man Man v. Self	Coming of Age Childhood v. Manhood	Classics Club DVD at CenterForLit website	*A Connecticut Yankee in King Arthur's Court,* Twain	3
Man v. Society Man v. Man Man v. Self	Sacrificial Love Bitterness & Revenge Faithfulness & Devotion Tyranny & Liberty	Teacher Guide at CenterForLit website	*A Wrinkle in Time,* L'Engle	4
Man v. Society Man v. Man	Social pressure to conform Persecution Forgiveness Coming of Age	Dialect, irony, foreshadowing, symbolism	*The Witch of Blackbird Pond*, Speare	5
Man v. Self Man v. Man	Good vs. Evil The sinful nature of man Repentance Honor Vanity/Pride vs. Humility	Symbolism	*Cheaper by the Dozen,* Gilbraith	6
Man v. Self Man v. Man Man v. Society	Greed vs. Contentment Faithfulness, Selflessness Appearances v. Realities Strength coming from Weakness Good v. Evil	*Ready Readers* at CenterForLit website	*The House of 60 Fathers*, Meindert de Jong	7
Man v. Self Man v. Nature	The Nature of Courage Coming of Age Superstition	Personification	*A Girl of the Limberlost,* Porter	8
Man v. Self Man v. God Man v. Nature	Perseverance/Patience Providence The nature of obstacles Puritan work ethic Faithfulness in little things	*Ready Readers* at CenterForLit website	*Banner in the Sky,* Ullman	9

9th Grade

Class	Title	Plot
1	*Owl Moon,* Yolen	A child experiences a family rite of passage when he goes owling with his father.
1	*All the Places to Love,* MacLachlan	A boy remembers all the places he's come to love and the people with whom they're associated, promising to share them with his new baby sister.
2	*The Aeneid ,* Virgil	Aeneas flees a burning Troy and journeys with other refugees to establish a new homeland on the coast of Italy.
3	*Sir Gawain and the Green Knight,* retold by Tolkien	Gawain, a knight of the renowned Round Table, finds his character and integrity tested when he accepts a challenge from a mysterious knight.
4	*Don Quixote (abridged),* Cervantes	A Spanish landowner, who spends his idle hours reading chivalric romances, fancies himself a knight. Engaging a squire with promises of a dukedom, he travels the countryside jousting at windmills and generally acting the fool in this classic satire.
5	*Romeo and Juliet,* Shakespeare	Impetuous teen lovers from feuding families forsake their parents' authority when they marry secretly; disaster ensues.
6	*Frankenstein,* Shelley	Scientific genius Victor Frankenstein seeks immortality by creating life. His creature does not meet expectations. The disastrous consequences that follow force us to face questions about the nature of man, God and Nature.
7	*The Strange Case of Dr. Jekyll and Mr. Hyde,* Stevenson	A narrator discovers that the respectable doctor he has long called his friend is also the mysterious menace who has committed a string of heinous crimes in late 19th century London.
8	*The Chosen ,* Potok	An unlikely friendship between two boys -- one an orthodox and the other a liberal Jew -- exposes cultural differences and leads to greater self-knowledge on the part of both friends.
9	*The Fellowship of the Ring ,* Tolkien	Young Frodo Baggins accepts a quest to destroy the Ring, whose power could destroy Middle Earth. Frodo is aided by a motley group of elves, dwarves and men - and by the mysterious wizard Gandalf.

Conflict	Theme	Aids/Devices	Alternate Title	Class
Man vs.Nature Man vs. Self	Self-control, Patience, Coming of Age	Imagery, Simile, Metaphor	*Sir Gawain and the Green Knight,* Morpurgo	1
Man vs. Nature	Generational heritage, the value of the land, mortality	*Ready Readers* at CenterForLit website	*Albert,* Napoli	1
Man v. Society Man v. Man Man v. the gods	Providence Patriotism - superiority of national to personal vision	Epic simile, alliteration, personification, allegory, irony	*The Prince and the Pauper,* Twain	2
Man v. Man Man v. Self	Importance of honor Importance of chastity Importance of self-control	Convention, metaphor, oxymoron, simile, symbolism	*The Black Arrow,* Stevenson	3
Man v. Self Man v. Society	Ridiculousness of chivalric romance Virtue, Morality, Goodness Realism vs. Idealism	The predecessor of the novel as a literary genre	*The Three Musketeers,* Dumas	4
Man v. Man Man v. God	Consequences of bitterness, and rashness Consequences of rebellion Dangers of deception Star crossed love	Poetic devices: blank verse, pun, irony, etc.	*Merchant of Venice,* Shakespeare	5
Man v. Nature Man v. God Man v. Man	What is a human being? Creature/Creator distinction	Flashback	*Good Morning, Miss Dove,* Patton	6
Man v. Man Man v. Self Man v. God Man v. Nature	Human Nature Original Sin Role of the Conscience Pride & Ambition	Foreshadowing	*The Black Falcon,* Sperry	7
Man v. Society Man v. Self	Coming of Age Faith vs. Religion Fathers and Sons	Symbolism, metaphor	*1984,* Orwell	8
Man v. Man Man v. Self Good vs. Evil	Seduction of ambition Strength in weakness Fellowship Sacrificial Love; Mercy Corruption of sin	Symbolism, foreshadowing	*The Two Towers,* Tolkien or *The Return of the King,* Tolkien	9

Class	Title	Plot
1	*Beowulf,* picture storybook	Beowulf the Geat, hero of his people, voyages to the land of king Hrothgar, to whom he owes a family debt. There he delivers Hrothgar's people from the monster scourge Grendel.
1	*Canterbury Tales,* retold by Barbara Cohen	An introduction to the famous tales of Geoffrey Chaucer, this book includes short re-tellings of the Nun's Priest's Tale, the Pardoner's Tale, the Wife of Bath's Tale and the Franklin's Tale.
2	*Beowulf*	Beowulf the Geat, hero of his people, voyages to the land of king Hrothgar, to whom he owes a family debt. There he delivers Hrothgar's people from the monster scourge Grendel.
3	*City of God,* Augustine (selections)	Genre: Philosophical Treatise (non-fiction). Augustine contends with accusations that Christians were responsible for the fall of Rome and exposes by reasonable argument the philosophical and spiritual folly of worshiping the gods.
4	*Divine Comedy: The Inferno,* Dante	Genre: Epic Poetry. In his middle age, the narrator, aided by the beautiful Beatrice and guided by the wise poet Virgil, travels through hell to understand the nature, breadth and consequences of sin.
5	*Canterbury Tales,* Chaucer (selections: General Prologue, Nun's Priest's Tale, Pardoner's Tale, Knight's Tale)	A diverse group of 14th century English men and women meet on a pilgrimage to the cathedral at Canterbury. They decide to pass time along the journey with a storytelling contest.
6	*The Taming of the Shrew,* Shakespeare	Genre: Play. Sharp-tongued Katerina meets her match when overbearing and shrewd Petrucchio weds and woos her.
7	*The Great Divorce,* Lewis	A day trip to the outer regions of Heaven gives inhabitants of Hell a once-in-a-lifetime opportunity: to experience paradise and its "Solid People" and choose their own citizenship.
8	*The Count of Monte Cristo,* Dumas	Unjustly imprisoned, the main character spends years plotting and then executing revenge upon those who ruined his life.
9	*The Hound of the Baskervilles,* Doyle	Sherlock Holmes disillusions spiritualists and uncovers a very material plot to kill Sir Henry Baskerville.

10th Grade

Monthly Model

Conflict	Theme	Aids/Devices	Alternate Title	Class
Man v. Animal/Monster, Man vs. Fate	Honor Good triumphs over evil The strength of virtue Fate	Kennings	*The Sign Painter,* Say	1
Conflicts vary, but all include Man v. Self, Man v. God	Human Nature Dangers of Pride, Greed Forgiving Debts	Allusion, irony, parody, allegory	*Chanticleer and the Fox,* Cooney	1
Man v. Animal/Monster, Man vs. Fate	Honor Good triumphs over evil The strength of virtue	Kennings	*Dream of the Rood* or Caedmon's *Hymn*	2
Christianity v. polytheism Man v. Society	Irrationality of pluralism Virtue Civic benefits of virtue (historical document)	Overstatement, apology, sarcasm	*Confessions,* Augustine (selections)	3
Man v. Self Man v. Man Man v. God	Fallen human nature Retributive Justice	Meter, epic simile, allegory, symbolism, allusion	*The Banquet,* Dante or *The Secret,* Petrarch	4
Every type of conflict is fully explored in this masterpiece	Human nature and its foibles The dangers of various character flaws Good triumphs over evil	Understatement, allegory, fable, irony	*Everyman,* Anonymous Medieval Drama	5
Man v. Man Man v. Self Man vs. Society	Marriage and male headship Love Authority and Submission Femininity Appearances vs. Reality	Blank verse, irony, pun	Alternate Shakespearean Comedies: *Midsummer Night's Dream or The Tempest*	6
Man v. Self Man v. God	Bitterness, salvation Vanity, vice Deception Pride	Teacher Guide at CenterForLit website	*Till We Have Faces,* Lewis or *The Screwtape Letters,* Lewis	7
Man v. Man Man v. Self	Injustice Revenge Bitterness and Hatred Deception	Symbolism, allusion	*The Three Musketeers,* Dumas	8
Man vs. Man Man vs. Self	Materialism Murder Superstition Rationalism	Red herring	The *Father Brown Mysteries,* GK Chesterton	9

Class	Title	Plot
1	*The Dangerous Journey*, Oliver Hunkin	An illustrated *Pilgrim's Progress* for children, this allegory follows a man, Christian, on his journey through life's perils to heaven's gates.
1	*Wilfrid Gordon Macdonald Partridge,* Fox	Wilfrid, a small boy, helps Miss Nancy, his elderly frend, find her memory.
2	*Paradise Lost*, Milton	The fallen angel, Lucifer, seeks revenge upon the Creator God by conducting a sneak attack on His newest creation, man.
3	*Hamlet,* Shakespeare	The noble prince of Denmark decides to avenge his father's murder, but struggles to make good on his pledge.
4	*Pilgrim's Progress*, Bunyan	Christian, tormented by spiritual anguish, follows his guide Evangelist on a journey from the City of Destruction to Mount Zion, the holy city
5	*Gulliver's Travels*, Swift (selections)	Gullible Gulliver's travels take him to curious kingdoms, each of which provides opportunities for him to see his own pride and foolishness.
6	*Faust,* Goethe (Book I)	Dr. Faust, unfulfilled by the wealth of knowledge he's gathered, sells his soul to the devil to obtain all his heart's desire.
7	*Bleak House*, Dickens	Orphan Esther Summerson seeks friendship and belonging among a family of Chancery suitors, while the noble Lady Dedlock struggles to protect a horrible secret.
8	*Wuthering Heights*, Bronte	A traveler uncovers the secret past of a wild and violent landowner, Heathcliff, and his one time beloved Kathy.
9	*Pride and Prejudice*, Austen	Elizabeth Bennet, jaded by Mr. Darcy's arrogance towards her, forms a prejudice against him that only desperate circumstances and valorous actions can overcome.

Conflict	Theme	Aids/Devices	Alternate Title	Class
Man vs. Man Man vs. Self Man vs. the World	Redemption, Grace, perseverance of the saints, the struggle against sin and the world	Allegory	*Three Names*, MacLachlan	1
Man vs. Nature Man vs. Self	The universal human experience The nature of friendship	*Ready Readers* at CenterForLit website	*The Tale of Meshka the Kvetch*, Chapman	1
Creature vs. Creator, Man vs. man	The Fall of Man Origins of Sin	Epic Simile, Epic devices	*Lycidas*, Milton	2
Man vs. Himself Man vs. Fate Man vs. Man	Human frailty The Tragic Hero Sanity vs. Insanity Revenge	Classics Club DVD at CenterForLit website	*Henry V*, Shakespeare	3
Man vs. Himself Man vs. Society Man vs. Man	Good vs. Evil Spiritual growth Salvation	Allegory	*The Importance of Being Earnest*, Wilde	4
Man vs. Man Man vs. Himself	The value of self-knowledge Humility	Allegory	*A Modest Proposal*, Swift	5
Man vs. God Man vs. Man Man vs. Self	Destructiveness of self-love Danger of Subverting Nature Perversity of Sin	Tragic Hero, irony, types, epic devices	*Alice in Wonderland*, Carroll	6
Man vs. Society Man vs. Man	Justice	Simile, personification, imagery	*David Copperfield*, Dickens	7
Man vs. Man Man vs. Society	Perverse love/Selfish love The nature of passion Revenge/Bitterness/Betrayal Manipulation Social Prejudice	Gothic Romance, symbolism, imagery	*The Dubliners*, Joyce	8
Man vs. Man Man vs. Society	Social Mores and Prejudices Honor/Virtue in both men and women	Irony (also makes use of satire)	*Jane Eyre*, Bronte	9

Class	Title	Plot
1	*The Man Who Walked Between the Towers,* Gerstein	True life narrative of the French tightrope artist who walked a wire strung between the historic twin towers.
1	*The Wall,* Sis	A Czechoslovakian boy grows up in a communist state.
2	*Last of the Mohicans* , Cooper	English soliders, American scouts and Mohican and Huron warriors engage in battle, intrigue and romance during the 18th century French and Indian War.
3	*Uncle Tom's Cabin,* Stowe	In spite of persecution, Tom, a Southern American black slave, continually proves himself heroic by selflessly sacrificing himself for others.
4	*The Scarlet Letter* , Hawthorne	American Puritan Hester Prynn and her illegitimate daughter Pearl suffer public shame for her adultery while the unnamed father remains hidden, bearing his guilt in secret.
5	*The Red Badge of Courage* , Crane	Young and naïve Henry joins the Union Army with visions of valour and heroism, but finds such valor impossible in a world without universal truth and meaning.
6	Hemingway Unit: *The Old Man and the Sea,* "Today Is Friday," "A Clean, Well-Lighted Place"	An old Cuban fisherman, Santiago, fallen on hard luck, hooks the largest fish of his career only to have it consumed by sharks before he can bring it to shore.
7	Flannery O'Connor short stories: *Revelation, A Good Man Is Hard to Find, The Lame Shall Enter First*	Upstanding, self-righteous Southerners encounter violent calamities that force them (and the reader) to consider the nature of man and the state of their souls.
8	*A Day In the Life of Ivan Denisovitch* , Solzhenitsyn	A Russian man struggles to retain his humanity in the face of the abuses of a Soviet concentration camp.
9	*To Kill A Mockingbird* , Lee	Two children, Scout and Jem, become both witnesses and victims to social bigotry and racism when their father, a court appointed lawyer, defends an innocent black man accused of raping a white woman.

Conflict	Theme	Aids/Devices	Alternate Title	Class
Man vs. Society Man vs Nature	Dreams/Visions Daring	Alliteration	*So Few Of Me*, Reynolds	1
Man vs. Society Man vs. Man Man vs. Nature	Freedom vs. Tyranny, the triumph of the human spirit	Imagery	*The Three Golden Keys*, Sis	1
Man vs. Man Man vs. Society Man vs. Nature Man vs. Fate	The "Noble Savage" Heroism Loyalty Revenge	Types, symbolism, imagery	*Heart of Darkness*, Conrad	2
Man vs. Man Man vs. Society	Self-Sacrificial Love Horrors Definition of Manhood Slavery vs. Freedom	Symbolism, monologue, allusion	*Rabble In Arms*, Roberts	3
Man vs. Society Man vs. Self Man vs. Man	Consequences of adultery (sin) Effects of unconfessed sin/guilty Revenge Slavery vs. Freedom	Symbolism	*The Last of the Mohicans*, Cooper	4
Man vs. Nature Man vs. Man Man vs. Self Man vs. Society	Mechanization of man Brutality of war The importance of empathy Determinism	Symbolism, imagery, metaphor, simile	*The Open Boat*, Crane	5
Man vs. Nature Man vs. Himself Man vs. Fate	Grace under pressure Empathy Disinterestedness of nature Courage in the face of a meaningless world	Symbolism, allusion	*The Pearl*, Steinbeck or *Of Mice and Men*, Steinbeck	6
Man vs. God Man vs. Man Man vs. Society Man vs. Himself	Human depravity Divine Grace Prejudice Self-righteousness	Irony	Edgar Allan Poe Shorts: *The Tell-Tale Heart, The Pit and the Pendulum, The Cask of Amontillado*	7
Man vs. Man Man vs. Society Man vs. Self	The indomitable human spirit Freedom vs. Tyranny Atrocity of Communism	Symbolism	*The Death of Ivan Ilyich*, Tolstoy	8
Man vs. Man Man vs. Society Man vs. Himself	Lost innocence Coming of Age Self-Sacrifical Love Racial Prejudice Source of Virtue/Honor	Symbolism, allusion, simile, metaphor	*The Call of the Wild*, London	9

Chapter 3

The Six Week Model

The Six Week Model

The Six Week Model of instruction follows the same methodology as the Monthly Model; the only difference between them is the number of books to be read and the number of meetings taken to discuss them. The Six-week Model is designed for smaller co-ops, single families, home schools conducting six or seven two-hour classes a year where Literature is part of a balanced approach to all subjects. Meeting format and preparation are similar to those described in the Monthly Model.

Kindergarten and First Grade:

The Six-Week Model works best with older elementary and high school students. This is because so much is attempted in a single meeting. Kindergartners' attention span is so short as to make a monthly meeting of sufficient length problematic. That's not to say younger students couldn't participate in a class of this kind. Should you wish to employ this model with K-2nd graders, scale back on your expectations. Realize however, that daily reading is a necessary part of early childhood development. Don't omit this, regardless of the model you might choose!

Choose 6 titles from your grade level reading list. In a class that is 1 hour in length, read the story aloud to the students. Classes 1-3, teach the students to identify the major story elements as follows:

Class 1 – Setting and Characters

Class 2 – Conflict and Plot

Class 3 – Themes and Literary Devices.

Class 4-6 - In the remaining sessions, utilize the plot chart and the method presented in *Teaching the Classics* basic seminar to lead the kids in reading and plotting stories on the plot chart to arrive at a discussion of basic themes. Crafts and activities may be developed to support the story presentation if time allows.

Second Grade:

Second graders will spend the first meeting learning to identify story elements and utilize the plot chart to arrive at a discussion of theme. Teachers will read aloud the picture books listed for Class 1, discussing them to present the elements of story. The remainder of the year, teachers will take up one story from the second grade list per class meeting, treating it in its entirety. In this way, the students will have read and discussed a total of 2 story books and 5 books at grade level by the end of the academic year. All reading from the main reading list will be done with parents outside of class. Classes will focus on comprehension and analysis rather than reading skills. Again, enrichment activities may be scheduled for each meeting (art projects, etc.) if time allows.

A sample schedule follows:

Class 1 – Read 2 picture story books and introduce story elements and plot chart.

Class 2 – Discuss book 1 in its entirety in a 1-2 hour class.

Class 3 – Discuss book 2 in its entirety in a 1-2 hour class.

Class 4 – Discuss book 3 in its entirety in a 1-2 hour class.

Class 5 – Discuss book 4 in its entirety in a 1-2 hour class.

Class 6 – Discuss book 5 in its entirety in a 1-2 hour class.

Third through Twelfth Grade:

Students in grades three through twelve will complete all readings in advance of the class meetings with the exception of the initial class, during which the discussion leader will read and discuss two picture books and present the model for analysis that will guide discussions for the remainder of the year. Each two hour class meeting that follows will treat one novel in its entirety. The class will cover six novels in full over the course of the academic year. A sample format follows:

Class 1 – Read aloud and discuss the two children's books suggested at the beginning of your grade level reading list. Take time to teach the elements of story as presented in the *Teaching the Classics* basic seminar. A sample schedule for the first meeting is below:

- Read picture book #1 and introduce the story elements of character, setting, conflict and plot.
- Plot the story on a plot chart. Introduce the 5th element of story, theme. Identify it.
- Using picture book #2, practice plotting the story on a plot chart, identifying elements of setting, character, conflict and any themes as they fit into the plot structure and events of the story.

Class 2 – Student should come to class having read the first title on the main reading list. Make sure students read the same edition and bring their copies to class. Discuss the story in one 2-hour discussion, leading the kids through the elements of story structure to arrive at a discussion of thematic ideas. Begin class with background information about the author and the period in which the story was written. Include any contextual details that might help them to understand the work more fully. Utilize the plot chart to encourage students to think carefully about the story's structure. Who is the main character? What is the main conflict? How is this resolved? Pay special attention to your placement of the climax as this will inform your understanding of the author's themes. Conflicts, conflict resolution, and themes are all intimately connected. Sometimes, there exists more than one possibility for the placement of the climax. Make students defend their choice with details from the text. How does this event resolve the greater story conflicts? What might the author be trying to say about his larger ideas by way of this? Utilize the Socratic List (located in the Appendix to the *Teaching the Classics* basic seminar) to stimulate discussion of the elements of story. Be sure to note any literary devices the author employed.

In particular, be sure to identify the following:

- Context
- Literary Devices
- Setting
- Characters
- Conflict
- Plot/Structural Elements
- Themes/Motifs

Repeat this type of discussion with a new title every six weeks to cover a total of 2 picture books and 6 novels in a nine month (36 week) academic year. As older students grow accustomed to the discussion, you can deepen your questioning by adding some elements of comparative or "worldview" analysis. For example, discuss how the stories answer the following questions:

- What's a good life?
- What good is life?
- What's a good death?
- What good is death?
- What's a good love?
- What good is love?[1]
- How do the author's answers to these questions compare with those of other works you've studied?
- How do his answers compare with your own ideas?

The Six-week Model adequately allows for the treatment of books at a basic level, with time for analysis, appreciation of stylistic devices and author's voice, and a book's place in the Western Canon.

---

[1] Thanks to Michael Bauman, Ph.D., our professor at Hillsdale College, who taught us to ask these questions back in 1989.

Class	Title	Plot
1	*The Bee Tree, Polacco*	A reluctant reader learns the sweetness of hard won success when her grandfather takes her on a bee hunt.
2	*The Tale of Peter Rabbit*, Potter	Peter disobeys his mother's order and sneaks into Mr. McGregor's garden, losing his new clothes and catching a terrible cold.
3	*Rainbow Fish*, Pfister	The lovely, rainbow-colored fish wins friends by sharing.
4	*Apples to Oregon*, Hopkinson	Daddy and Delicious embark on a journey from Iowa to Oregon with a "nursery" wagon full of fruit trees and hearts full of hope.
5	*Peter and the Wolf*, Prokofiev	When Peter goes beyond the garden gate, he is stalked by a ravenous wolf.
6	*The Keeping Quilt*, Polacco	An immigrant family preserves its heritage and memories in a special keepsake: a quilt that becomes a family heirloom.

Conflict	Theme	Aids/Devices	Alternate Title	Class
Man vs. Nature, Man vs. Self	Rewards of patience and perseverance, the sweetness of success	Alliteration, Dialect, Symbolism	*Why Mosquitoes Buzz in People's Ears*, Aardema	1
Man vs. Man, Man vs. Nature	Consequences of disobedience	*Teaching the Classics* basic seminar	*The Tale of Benjamin Bunny*, Potter	2
Man vs. Self	Self-sacrifice, sharing	Circumstantial irony	*Just Plain Fancy*, Polacco	3
Man vs. Nature	Determination, perseverance, cooperation, vision	*Ready Readers* at CenterForLit website	*King Bidgood's In the Bathtub*, Wood	4
Man vs. Nature	Man's dominion over nature	Anthropomorphism	*The Whispering Rabbit*, Brown	5
Man vs. Nature	The preservation of heritage and family in the face of time's passage	Symbolism	*Thank You, Mr. Falker*, Polacco	6

1st Grade

Class	Title	Plot
1	*The Story of Ferdinand,* Leaf	Unlike the other bulls, Ferdinand refuses to fight in the bullfights in Madrid, preferring peaceful contemplation in his meadow.
2	*Brave Irene,* Steig	When her seamstress mother is taken ill, young Irene braves a snowstorm to deliver a gown commissioned by the duchess.
3	*A Bargain for Frances,* Hoban	Frances, swindled by her friend Thelma, gets even.
4	*The Gardener,* Stewart	Lydia Grace Finch leaves her family to live with her uncle during the Great Depression.
5	*Horton Hears a Who,* Seuss	Horton the elephant hears tiny voices on a floating dust mote and struggles to protect the tiny lives they represent in spite of his skeptical, scoffing neighbors.
6	*The Biggest Bear,* Ward	When little Johnny's pet bear cub grows to become a neghborhood nuisance, he must make a man's decision.

Conflict	Theme	Aids/Devices	Alternate Title	Class
Man vs Man, Man vs. Nature	Pacifism, individuality	Teacher Guide at CenterForLit website	*The Church Mouse,* Graham	1
Man vs. Nature, Man vs. Self	Bravery, determination, loyalty, integrity	*Ready Readers* at CenterForLit website	*The Wing Shop ,* Woodruff	2
Man vs. Man	Friendship, shrewdness, coming of age	Auido Lecture at CenterForLit website	*The Fool of the World and the Flying Ship,* Ransome	3
Man vs. Society, Man vs. Self, Man vs. Man	Bloom where you are planted. The value of beauty. Grace.	Teacher Guide at CenterForLit website	*The Empty Pot ,* Demi	4
Man vs. Society	Sanctity of life, Faith, Persecution	Rhyme	*The Stranger ,* VanAllsburg	5
Man vs. Nature, Man vs. Self, Man vs. Man	Meaning of manhood, courage; Coming of Age	Understatement	*Caps For Sale ,* Slobodkina	6

Class	Title	Plot
1	*Amos and Boris, Steig*	The story of an unlikely friendship between a mouse and a whale reminiscient of Aesop's fable of the mouse and the lion.
1	*Thunder Cake,* Polacco	Babushka decides to cure her granddaughter of cowardice by making her face some of her fears.
2	*Mouse Soup* , Lobel	Shrewd Mouse invents stories to entertain Weasel and escape becoming his dinner.
3	*My Father's Dragon* , Gannet	The narrator relates the story of his clever father, Elmer Elevator, who journeys to the land of Tangerina to free a dragon who's been enslaved by the other islanders.
4	*The Bears On Hemlock Mountain* , Dagliesh	When a young boy travels over the mountain on an errand for his mother, he discovers that there **are** bears on Hemlock Mountain.
5	*The Minstrel In the Tower,* Skurzynski	Alice and Roger, siblings, travel by foot to find their estranged uncle and bring him to their sick mother's aid; a lute adorned with an eagle is the only proof of their identities.
6	*The Matchlock Gun* , Edmonds	Young Edward, his mother and his little sister must protect themselves from unfriendly indians while father is away fighting with the militia.

Conflict	Theme	Aids/Devices	Alternate Title	Class
Man vs. Nature	Kindness remembered, friendship	Alliteration, Anthropomorphism	*Tops and Bottoms*, Stevens	1
Man vs. Nature, Man vs. Self	Bravery, Love	Sensory Language, Repetition	*Blueberries for Sal, McCloskey*	1
Man vs. Man	Mouse proves the value of reading and thinking in this humorous tale; shrewdness.	Story frame	*The 100 Dresses*, Estes	2
Man vs. Nature, Man vs. Society	Forethought, kindness, friendship, compassion, loyalty	Alliteration	*Benjamin West and His Cat, Grimalkin,* Henry	3
Man vs. Nature, Man vs. Self	Courage and responsibility, actions and consequences	Foreshadowing, imagery, repetition	*Stuart Little,* White	4
Man vs. Man, Man vs. Nature	The enduring love of family	Symbolism	*A Bear Called Paddington*, Bond (Since this book is episodic, chapters can be studied in isolation.)	5
Man vs. Man, Man vs Self	Courage, obedience, coming of age	Foreshadowing	*Billy Blaze adventures,*	6

Class	Title	Plot
1	*Winnie the Pooh, "The House at Pooh Corner - In Which Eeyore Finds the Wolery and Owl Moves Into It",* Milne	When Owl loses his home to a wind storm, the other residents of the 100 acre wood help him relocate.
1	*Horton Hears A Who*, Seuss	Horton's keen ears hear better than most and make him alone responsible for protecting the wee people of Who-ville from annihilation.
2	*The Cricket In Times Square*, Selden	Chester the cricket and Mario the newsboy learn the self-sacrificial nature of real friendship as they endeavor to care for one another.
3	*The Mouse and the Motorcycle,* Cleary	Ralph, a mouse who lives in a roadside inn with his family, befriends and saves the life of a young boy, who rewards him with a gift of a toy motorcycle.
4	*Misty of Chincoteague*, Henry	Paul and Maureen Bibee work hard to earn money to buy the famous Phantom and her colt at the yearly pony auction on Chincoteague Island.
5	*The Hundred Dresses*, Estes	Maggie, horrified when her silent complicity to classroom bigotry forces classmate Wanda from town, must live with her guilt and the unanswered question of Wanda's fate.
6	*The Cabin Faced West,* Fritz	Ten year old Ann Hamilton, a dissatisfied and lonely pioneer girl in Pennsylvania, learns the satisfaction hard labor brings and becomes personally invested in her family's pioneer vision.
7	*Charlotte's Web*, White	When Fern's petted piglet Wilbur moves to the barn, his loneliness and fears are abated by his friendship with Charlotte, a sagacious grey barn spider.

3rd Grade

Conflict	Theme	Aids/Devices	Alternate Title	Class
Man vs. Nature Man vs. Man Man vs. Self	Self-sacrificial love and friendship	Personification	*Pippi Longstocking*, Lindgren	1
Man vs. Man Man vs. Society	Self-Sacrifice, Mob violence, the Value of life ("A person's a person no matter how small!")	Rhyme	*The Boxcar Children*, Warner	1
Man vs. Nature Man vs. Self	The nature of friendship; the importance of freedom	*Ready Readers* at CenterForLit website	*Henry and Ribsy*, Cleary	2
Man vs. Nature Man vs. Man Man vs. Self	Personal responsibility, courage, friendship	Alliteration, assonance, onomatopoeia, anthropomorphism	*Homer Price*, McCloskey	3
Man vs. Nature Man vs. Self Man vs. Man	Stewardship/Dominion Mandate; Selfishness vs Selflessness; Sacrificial love; Coming of Age	*Ready Readers* at CenterForLit website	*The Great Brain*, Fitzgerald	4
Man vs. Man Man vs. Self Man vs. Society	Racism, Guilt, Complicity, Consequences, It is better to suffer a wrong than to do one.	Alliteration	*The Mouse of Amherst*, Spires (together with the poetry of Emily Dickinson)	5
Man vs. Nature Man vs. Self	Suffering and hardship produce character and fruitfulness; westward expansion	Symbolism, assonance, alliteration	*Stuart Little*, White	6
Man vs. Nature Man vs. Self Man vs. Man	Self-Sacrificial love and friendship: "Greater love has no man than this, that he would lay down his life for a friend."	Anthropomorphism	*A Little Princess*, Burnett	7

4th Grade

Class	Title	Plot
1	*Bedtime For Frances,* Hoban	Frances, a badger, hates bedtime and does her best to delay it.
1	*Apples To Oregon,* Hopkinson	Delicious and her daddy are determined to move their family and their orchard to the temperate state of Oregon.
2	*Mr. Popper's Penguins*, Atwater	When Mr. Popper, a poor housepainter with big dreams, receives penguins by post from an Arctic explorer, he devises a plan by which to provide for both them and his family.
3	*Wind In the Willows,* Grahame	Fickle Mr. Toad of Toad Hall becomes entranced by the faddish new motorcar; his friends endeavor to recall him to his senses and restore to him his dignity and place in the community.
4	*Charlie and the Chocolate Factory*, Dahl	When Charlie Bucket discovers a golden ticket in his Wonka Bar, he embarks on an adventure that tests his character and reveals his personal integrity.
5	*Trumpet of the Swan,* White	Louis, a swan born mute, learns to communicate by means of a trumpet that his father steals from a local music store; with the trumpet, he earns enough money to repay his father's debt to the store owner.
6	*Snow Treasure*, McSwigan	The children of a town occupied by Nazis during WWII are given the important responsibility of smuggling the national treasure out of the country.
7	*Miracle On Maple Hill*, Sorenson	A young girl and her family return to her mother's childhood home on Maple Hill in search of rest and respite for their father, a recovered POW.

Conflict	Theme	Aids/Devices	Alternate Title	Class
Man vs. Man Man vs. Self	Obedience, consequences	Rhyme, onomatopoeia	*Roxaboxen,* Cohen	1
Man vs. Nature Man vs. Society Man vs. Self	Determination, Cooperation, Vision, Westward Expansion, the Pioneer Spirit, Industry	*Ready Readers* at CenterForLit website	*Stellaluna,* Canon	1
Man vs. Nature	Ingenuity, Singlemindedness, Vision	Alliteration	*The Jungle Books*, Kipling	2
Man vs. Man Man vs. Society Man vs. Self	City vs. Country, Industrialization, Urbanization, Value of community, Social Hierarchy, True Friendship	Classics Club DVD at CenterforLit website	*Owls In the Family*, Mowat	3
Man vs. Society Man vs. Self Man vs. Man	Value of personal integrity, Honesty, Deception	Rhyme, symbolism	*The Penderwicks,* Birdsall	4
Man vs. Man Man vs. Self Man vs. Nature	Character qualities such as determination, integrity, commitment, ethics; remuneration; fatherly love	*Ready Readers* at CenterForLit website	*Swiss Family Robinson*, Wyss	5
Man vs. Society Man vs. Man Man vs. Self	Bravery, patriotism, leadership, self-control	Personification, allusion	*The Whipping Boy*, Fleischman	6
Man vs. Society Man vs. Self Man vs. Nature	Regeneration/Renewal, Value of Community, Coming of Age/Growing Up	*Ready Readers* at CenterForLit website	*Five Children and It*, Nesbit	7

Class	Title	Plot
1	*Why Mosquitoes Buzz In People's Ears,* Aardema	In this African fable, a mosquito's foolishness touches off an unexpected, tragic chain of events.
1	*Chrysanthemum,* Henkes	Chrysanthemum overcomes peer teasing and learns to love her name.
2	*A Door In the Wall* , DeAngeli	Robin, a young nobleman's son, is struck with paralysis and abandoned by his household; a monk nurses him to health and teaches him self-discipline, industry, and respect for others.
3	Shakespeare Intro using Lamb's Tales, "Macbeth" and the original play *Macbeth,* Shakespeare	When noble Macbeth, tempted by evil spirits, murders his kinsman and king, he finds he may keep his ill-gotten crown only through further bloodshed.
4	*Straw Into Gold,* Schmidt	Drawing on the timeless fairytale of *Rumplestiltskin,* this story provides a reason for the little man's seemingly capricious act.
5	*The Chronicles of Narnia* , Lewis	The Pevensie children stumble into another land by way of an enchanted wardrobe and come to know not only themselves, but also the Lord of the land, Aslan, and the nature of love.
6	*The Indian in theCupboard* , Banks	Omri discovers that the old cupboard his brother gives him for his birthday has magical abilities to turn toys into living creatures, but he's unprepared for the implications of this lifegiving power.
7	*The Tale of Desperaux* , DiCamillo	Desperaux, the only mouse to survive from his litter, perpetually disappoints both his French mother and the rest of the mouse community with his nonconformity; still, he survives this rejection and fulfills his purpose providentially.

5th Grade

Conflict	Theme	Aids/Devices	Alternate Title	Class
Man vs. Man Man vs. Himself	Actions have consequences.	Onomatopoeia	*The Apple and the Arrow*, Buff	1
Man vs. Man Man vs. Himself	Self-confidence, Fear of Man, Peer problems, envy/jealousy	Pun	*King Arthur The Sword in the Stone*, Talbott	1
Man vs. God Man vs. Self Man vs. Nature Man vs. Society	Goodness and character are born through suffering. Providence. Grace	*Ready Readers* at CenterForLit website	*From the Mixed Up Files of Mrs. Basil E. Frankweiler*, Konigsburg	2
Man vs. Self Man vs. Society Man vs. Man Man vs. Fate	Sin Nature (Fatal Flaw), Deceitfulness of the human heart, Dangers of selfish ambition	Poetic devices, blank verse, pun, double entendre	*The Invention of Hugo Cabret*, Selznick	3
Man vs. Man Man vs. Society Man vs. Self Man vs. Providence	Selfless Love, Comparison and discussion of strength and weakness, Providence, Appearance vs. Reality	Frame, Imagery, Foreshadowing, Sensory Language	*Soup,* Robert Newton Peck	4
Man vs. Man Man vs. Self Man vs. Society Man vs. God	Sin Nature of Man, Sacrificial Love and Substitutionary Atonement, Redemption, the effects of Envy, Betrayal	Frame, Symbolism, Anthropomorphism	*Voyage of the Dawn Treader*, Lewis	5
Man vs. Self Man vs. Man Man vs. God	The nature of human life and responsibility.	Foreshadowing	*The Silver Chair*, Lewis	6
Man vs. Society Man vs. Self Man vs. Man	Betrayal ("perfidy"), providence, social pressure/prejudice, individuality, courtly love, and honor.	Symbolism, Alliteration, Imagery	*Beauty,* McKinley	7

Class	Title	Plot
1	*The Gardener*, Stewart	Lydia Grace must leave her family and live with her uncle in the city during the depression; her cheerful countenance and graciousness make her a blessing to everyone around her.
1	*Paul Revere's Ride,* Longfellow	The great American Poet Laureate tells the story of Paul Revere's famous ride to alert the Minutemen of the British soldiers' approach on the eve of the battle of Lexington & Concord in 1775.
2	*Tuck Everlasting,* Babbitt	A young girl befriends the Tuck family, who have accidentally discovered the fountain of youth. She must decide whether to live a natural life herself and how to help them keep their secret from those who would exploit it.
3	*Julius Caesar,* Shakespeare	Brutus, Cassius and the other conspirators plot and perform the assassination of Julius Caesar. They then fight with the Triumvirate for control of Rome, only to find that the ambitious spirit for which they killed Caesar dwells in their own hearts as well.
4	*The Adventures of Tom Sawyer, Twain*	Mischievous Tom "plays, fights and hides" his way through childhood in small town Missouri, searching for hidden treasure and narrowly escaping the clutches of the evil Injun Joe.
5	*At the Back of the North Wind,* MacDonald	A sickly boy journeys with the mythical North Wind to faraway lands and learns of her trustworthiness, faithfulness and love.
6	*I Am David,* Holm	Young David, who has lived his whole life separated from his parents in a Nazi concentration camp, escapes with the help of a prison guard and must walk north across Europe to find freedom and happiness.
7	*Treasure Island,* Stevenson	Jim Hawkins, whose family is deeply in debt, discovers a pirate's treasure map and embarks on a dangerous journey to find the treasure, encountering honest men and ruffians in equal measure along the way.

Conflict	Theme	Aids/Devices	Alternate Title	Class
Man vs. Society Man vs. Man Man vs. Self	Bloom where you are planted A cheerful heart does good like a medicine	Teacher Guide at CenterForLit website	*The Friend* , Stewart	1
Man v. Man Man v. Society	Patriotism Liberty	*Teaching the Classics* basic seminar	*The Old Woman Who Named Things* , Rylant	1
Man v. Nature Man v. Man Man v. Self	The story explores the natural order of things and the consequences of upsetting this order.	Symbolism, Imagery	*Anne of Green Gables,* Montgomery	2
Man v. Man Man v. Self Man v. Society	The wickedness of the human heart The law of sowing and reaping Tyranny Ambition Frailty	*Ready Readers* at CenterForLit website	*Mrs. Frisbee & the Rats of NIMH,* O'Brien	3
Man v. Man Man v. Nature	A reminiscence of boyhood The wonder of childhood Human nature	Irony, Allusion	*Black Ships Before Troy,* Sutcliffe	4
Man v. God Man v. Man	This allegory explores the problem of pain and the nature of death while depicting goodness, kindness and charity.	*Ready Readers* at CenterForLit website	*A Girl of the Limberlost,* Porter	5
Man v. Man Man v. Society	Sacrificial love Faith, Hope and Trust Determination	Symbolism	*The Witch of Blackbird Pond,* Speare	6
Man v. Man Man v. Self	Coming of Age Shrewdness/Resourcefulness Honesty Mercy Friendship	*Ready Readers* at CenterForLit website	*The Pushcart War,* Merrill	7

Class	Title	Plot
1	*Amos & Boris,* Steig	When the mouse Amos's ship capsizes, he is rescued by the whale Boris; years later, Amos returns the favor unexpectedly.
1	*A Bargain for Frances,* Hoban	When Frances's friend Thelma takes advantage of her, Frances finds a way to get even.
2	*The Bronze Bow*, Speare	Daniel bar-Jamin, a rugged runaway who has cast his lot with the zealots, is recalled to responsibility by his grandmother's death. He must wrestle with his hatred for the Romans who occupy Israel and his growing love for his people.
3	*The Odyssey,* Homer	Odysseus, who has struggled 10 years in the Trojan war and been delayed from homecoming another 10 years for offending the gods, finally regains his home.
4	*Huckleberry Finn,* Twain	Vagabond Huck and runaway slave Jim try to escape society by floating down the Mississippi River on a raft.
5	*Great Expectations*, Dickens	When the impoverished orphan Pip discovers that he has come into an inheritance from a mysterious benefactor, he distances himself from his humble friends and family to better himself and earn the love of the wealthy and beautiful Estella.
6	*Watership Down*, Adams	When Hazel's brother, Fiver, predicts doom for their warren, Hazel leads a group of their friends into the wilderness to establish a new home on Watership Down.
7	*The Hiding Place*, Ten Boom	The true story of Corrie Ten Boom and her family, who are caught sheltering Jews from the Nazis in WWII Holland. They are arrested and sent to a concentration camp, where they must struggle to survive.

7th Grade

Conflict	Theme	Aids/Devices	*Alternate Title*	Class
Man v. Nature	Friendship Kindness Faithfulness & Loyalty	Descriptive language, Irony	*Casey At the Bat,* retold by Polacco	1
Man v. Man Man v. Self	Deception Shrewdness Friendship Coming of Age	Audio Lecture at CenterForLit website	*Thunder Cake,* Polacco	1
Man v. Society Man v. Self Man v. God	Bitterness & its Effects The nature of forgiveness Sacrificial love Redemption	*Ready Readers* at CenterForLit website	*The Devil's Arithmetic,* Yolen	2
Man v. gods Man v. Man	The importance of marriage and family Faithfulness Patriotism and loyalty Justice	Epic Simile	*The Wanderings of Odysseus,* Sutcliffe (a re-telling of The Odyssey for young readers)	3
Man v. Sociey Man v. Man Man v. Self	Freedom & Slavery Character & Integrity Racism Pride vs. Humility Social Conventions	Classics Club DVD at CenterForLit website	*Henry V,* Shakespeare	4
Man v. Self Man v. Man Man vs. Society	Redemptive Love Pride vs. Humility Appearance vs. Reality Fear of Man; Bitterness Coming of Age; Friendship	Symbolism, imagery, allegory, foreshadowing	*Kidnapped,* Stevenson	5
Man v. Society Man v. Nature [Man v. Man/Self]	A study of human Totalitarianism Tyranny vs. Freedom Leadership Faith, Fear, Bravery	Anthropomorphism, Foreshadowing	*Here There Be Dragons,* Owen	6
Man v. Society Man v. Self Man v. God Man v. Man	Redemptive Love God's grace & sovereignty Forgiveness Bitterness The sinful nature of man	Foreshadowing, irony	*The 100 Cupboards,* Wilson	7

Class	Title	Plot
1	*The Biggest Bear,* Ward	A young boy must rid the neighborhood of his beloved pet bear, who has become a nuisance.
1	*Letting Swift River Go,* Yolen	Visiting the inundated Swift River Valley which once was her home, Sally Jane makes peace with her drowned past.
2	*The Iliad,* Homer	Greek warrior and demi-god Achilles, embittered by King Agamemnon's ill treatment, refuses to reconcile and withdraws from the battle between the Greeks and the Trojans.
3	*The Yearling,* Rawlings	Jody must give up his childhood and embrace the responsibilities of a man when his pet fawn grows up to menace the family farm.
4	*A Tale of Two Cities,* Dickens	Exiled aristocrat Charles Darnay returns to France during the Reign of Terror; without the aid of family friend Sydney Carton, he will be executed, leaving his family desolate.
5	*The Hobbit,* Tolkien	Homebody Bilbo Baggins is petitioned by the wizard Gandalf to accompany a group of dwarves on a mission to burgle stolen treasure from the evil dragon Smaug.
6	*Call it Courage,* Sperry	A young boy must master his fear of the sea in this coming-of-age adventure.
7	*Carry On, Mr. Bowditch,* Latham	Nathaniel Bowditch is a math whiz and longs to be a Harvard man;. his apprenticeship forces him to "sail by ash breeze," gaining him character, achievement and acclaim.

8th Grade

Six Week Model

Conflict	Theme	Aids/Devices	Alternate Title	Class
Man v. Nature Man v. Self Man v. Society	Manhood/Masculinity What is courage? Self-denial What is strength?	Pun, parody, irony, understatement	*Mirette On the High Wire*, McCulley	1
Man v. Society Man v. Nature Man v. Self	The nature of time Bitterness & forgiveness Link between acceptance & peace	*Ready Readers* at CenterForLit website	*Angelo*, Macaulay	1
Man v. Man Man v. Self Man v. gods	Bitterness & its consequences Honor Pride Loyalty & Friendship	Epic Simile, *In Medias Res*	*Black Ships Before Troy*, Sutcliffe (a re-telling of the Iliad for children)	2
Man v. Nature Man v. Man Man v. Self	Coming of Age Childhood v. Manhood	Classics Club DVD at CenterForLit website	*A Connecticut Yankee in King Arthur's Court*, Twain	3
Man v. Society Man v. Man Man v. Self	Sacrificial Love Bitterness & Revenge Faithfulness & Devotion Tyranny & Liberty	Teacher Guide at CenterForLit website	*A Wrinkle in Time*, L'Engle	4
Man v. Self Man v. Man Man v. Society	Greed vs. Contentment Faithfulness, Selflessness Appearances v. Realities Strength coming from Weakness Good v. Evil	*Ready Readers* at CenterForLit website	*The House of 60 Fathers*, Meindert de Jong	5
Man v. Self Man v. Nature	The Nature of Courage Coming of Age Superstition	Personification	*A Girl of the Limberlost*, Porter	6
Man v. Self Man v. God Man v. Nature	Perseverance/Patience Providence The nature of obstacles Puritan work ethic Faithfulness in little things	*Ready Readers* at CenterForLit website	*Banner in the Sky*, Ullman	7

Class	Title	Plot
1	*Owl Moon,* Yolen	A child experiences a family rite of passage when he goes owling with his father.
1	*All the Places to Love,* MacLachlan	A boy remembers all the places he's come to love and the people with whom they're associated, promising to share them with his new baby sister.
2	*The Aeneid,* Virgil	Aeneas flees a burning Troy and journeys with other refugees to establish a new homeland on the coast of Italy.
3	*Sir Gawain and the Green Knight,* retold by Tolkien	Gawain, a knight of the renowned Round Table, finds his character and integrity tested when he accepts a challenge from a mysterious knight.
4	*Romeo and Juliet,* Shakespeare	Impetuous teen lovers from feuding families forsake their parents' authority when they marry secretly; disaster ensues.
5	*Frankenstein,* Shelley	Scientific genius Victor Frankenstein seeks immortality by creating life. His creature does not meet expectations. The disastrous consequences that follow force us to face questions about the nature of man, God and Nature.
6	*The Strange Case of Dr. Jekyll and Mr. Hyde,* Stevenson	A narrator discovers that the respectable doctor he has long called his friend is also the mysterious menace who has committed a string of heinous crimes in late 19th century London.
7	*The Chosen,* Potok	An unlikely friendship between two boys -- one an orthodox and the other a liberal Jew -- exposes cultural differences and leads to greater self-knowledge on the part of both friends.

Conflict	Theme	Aids/Devices	Alternate Title	Class
Man vs.Nature Man vs. Self	Self-control, Patience, Coming of Age	Imagery, Simile, Metaphor	*Sir Gawain and the Green Knight,* Morpurgo	1
Man vs. Nature	Generational heritage, the value of the land, mortality	*Ready Readers* at CenterForLit website	*Albert,* Napoli	1
Man v. Society Man v. Man Man v. the gods	Providence Patriotism - superiority of national to personal vision	Epic simile, alliteration, personification, allegory, irony	*The Prince and the Pauper,* Twain	2
Man v. Man Man v. Self	Importance of honor Importance of chastity Importance of self-control	Convention, metaphor, oxymoron, simile, symbolism	*The Black Arrow,* Stevenson	3
Man v. Man Man v. God	Consequences of bitterness, and rashness Consequences of rebellion Dangers of deception Star crossed love	Poetic devices: blank verse, pun, irony, etc.	*Merchant of Venice,* Shakespeare	4
Man v. Nature Man v. God Man v. Man	What is a human being? Creature/Creator distinction	Flashback	*Good Morning, Miss Dove,* Patton	5
Man v. Man Man v. Self Man v. God Man v. Nature	Human Nature Original Sin Role of the Conscience Pride & Ambition	Foreshadowing	*The Black Falcon,* Sperry	6
Man v. Society Man v. Self	Coming of Age Faith vs. Religion Fathers and Sons	Symbolism, metaphor	*1984,* Orwell	7

Class	Title	Plot
1	*Beowulf,* picture storybook	Beowulf the Geat, hero of his people, voyages to the land of king Hrothgar, to whom he owes a family debt. There he delivers Hrothgar's people from the monster scourge Grendel.
1	*Canterbury Tales,* retold by Barbara Cohen	An introduction to the famous tales of Geoffrey Chaucer, this book includes short re-tellings of the Nun's Priest's Tale, the Pardoner's Tale, the Wife of Bath's Tale and the Franklin's Tale.
2	*Beowulf*	Beowulf the Geat, hero of his people, voyages to the land of king Hrothgar, to whom he owes a family debt. There he delivers Hrothgar's people from the monster scourge Grendel.
3	*Divine Comedy: The Inferno,* Dante	Genre: Epic Poetry. In his middle age, the narrator, aided by the beautiful Beatrice and guided by the wise poet Virgil, travels through hell to understand the nature, breadth and consequences of sin.
4	*Canterbury Tales,* Chaucer (selections: General Prologue, Nun's Priest's Tale, Pardoner's Tale, Knight's Tale)	A diverse group of 14th century English men and women meet on a pilgrimage to the cathedral at Canterbury. They decide to pass time along the journey with a storytelling contest.
5	*The Taming of the Shrew,* Shakespeare	Genre: Play. Sharp-tongued Katerina meets her match when overbearing and shrewd Petrucchio weds and woos her.
6	*The Great Divorce,* Lewis	A day trip to the outer regions of Heaven gives inhabitants of Hell a once-in-a-lifetime opportunity: to experience paradise and its "Solid People" and choose their own citizenship.
7	*The Hound of the Baskervilles,* Doyle	Sherlock Holmes disillusions spiritualists and uncovers a very material plot to kill Sir Henry Baskerville.

Conflict	Theme	Aids/Devices	Alternate Title	Class
Man v. Animal/Monster, Man vs. Fate	Honor Good triumphs over evil The strength of virtue Fate	Kennings	*The Sign Painter,* Say	1
Conflicts vary, but all include Man v. Self, Man v. God	Human Nature Dangers of Pride, Greed Forgiving Debts	Allusion, irony, parody, allegory	*Chanticleer and the Fox,* Cooney	1
Man v. Animal/Monster, Man vs. Fate	Honor Good triumphs over evil The strength of virtue	Kennings	*Dream of the Rood* or Caedmon's *Hymn*	2
Man v. Self Man v. Man Man v. God	Fallen human nature Retributive Justice	Meter, epic simile, allegory, symbolism, allusion	*The Banquet,* Dante or *The Secret,* Petrarch	3
Every type of conflict is fully explored in this masterpiece	Human nature and its foibles The dangers of various character flaws Good triumphs over evil	Understatement, allegory, fable, irony	*Everyman,* Anonymous Medieval Drama	4
Man v. Man Man v. Self Man vs. Society	Marriage and male headship Love Authority and Submission Femininity Appearances vs. Reality	Blank verse, irony, pun	Alternate Shakespearean Comedies: *Midsummer Night's Dream or The Tempest*	5
Man v. Self Man v. God	Bitterness, salvation Vanity, vice Deception Pride	Teacher Guide at CenterForLit website	*Till We Have Faces,* Lewis or *The Screwtape Letters,* Lewis	6
Man vs. Man Man vs. Self	Materialism Murder Superstition Rationalism	Red herring	The *Father Brown Mysteries,* GK Chesterton	7

Class	Title	Plot
1	*The Dangerous Journey* , Oliver Hunkin	An illustrated *Pilgrim's Progres* s for children, this allegory follows a man, Christian, on his journey through life's perils to heaven's gates.
1	*Wilfrid Gordon Macdonald Partridge,* Fox	Wilfrid, a small boy, helps Miss Nancy, his elderly frend, find her memory.
2	*Paradise Lost* , Milton	The fallen angel, Lucifer, seeks revenge upon the Creator God by conducting a sneak attack on His newest creation, man.
3	*Hamlet,* Shakespeare	The noble prince of Denmark decides to avenge his father's murder, but struggles to make good on his pledge.
4	*Gulliver's Travels* , Swift (selections)	Gullible Gulliver's travels take him to curious kingdoms, each of which provides opportunities for him to see his own pride and foolishness.
5	*Faust,* Goethe (Book I)	Dr. Faust, unfulfilled by the wealth of knowledge he's gathered, sells his soul to the devil to obtain all his heart's desire.
6	*Bleak House* , Dickens	Orphan Esther Summerson seeks friendship and belonging among a family of Chancery suitors, while the noble Lady Dedlock struggles to protect a horrible secret.
7	*Wuthering Heights* , Bronte	A traveler uncovers the secret past of a wild and violent landowner, Heathcliff, and his one time beloved Kathy.

Conflict	Theme	Aids/Devices	Alternate Title	Class
Man vs. Man Man vs. Self Man vs. the World	Redemption, Grace, perseverance of the saints, the struggle against sin and the world	Allegory	*Three Names*, MacLachlan	1
Man vs. Nature Man vs. Self	The universal human experience The nature of friendship	*Ready Readers* at CenterForLit website	*The Tale of Meshka the Kvetch*, Chapman	1
Creature vs. Creator, Man vs. man	The Fall of Man Origins of Sin	Epic Simile, Epic devices	*Lycidas,* Milton	2
Man vs. Himself Man vs. Fate Man vs. Man	Human frailty The Tragic Hero Sanity vs. Insanity Revenge	Classics Club DVD at CenterForLit website	*Henry V,* Shakespeare	3
Man vs. Man Man vs. Himself Man vs. Society	The value of self-knowledge Humility Creaturehood of man	Allegory	*A Modest Proposal*, Swift	4
Man vs. God Man vs. Man Man vs. Self	Destructiveness of self-love Danger of Subverting Nature Perversity of Sin	Tragic Hero, irony, types, epic devices	*Alice in Wonderland*, Carroll	5
Man vs. Society Man vs. Man	Justice	Simile, personification, imagery	*David Copperfield*, Dickens	6
Man vs. Man Man vs. Society	Perverse love/Selfish love The nature of passion Revenge/Bitterness/Betrayal Manipulation Social Prejudice	Gothic Romance, symbolism, imagery	*The Dubliners*, Joyce	7

Class	Title	Plot
1	*The Man Who Walked Between the Towers,* Gerstein	True life narrative of the French tightrope artist who walked a wire strung between the historic twin towers.
1	*The Wall,* Sis	A Czechoslovakian boy grows up in a communist state.
2	*Last of the Mohicans ,* Cooper	English soliders, American scouts and Mohican and Huron warriors engage in battle, intrigue and romance during the 18th century French and Indian War.
3	*The Scarlet Letter ,* Hawthorne	American Puritan Hester Prynn and her illegitimate daughter Pearl suffer public shame for her adultery while the unnamed father remains hidden, bearing his guilt in secret.
4	*The Red Badge of Courage ,* Crane	Young and naïve Henry joins the Union Army with visions of valour and heroism, but finds such valor impossible in a world without universal truth and meaning.
5	Hemingway Unit: *The Old Man and the Sea,* "Today Is Friday," "A Clean, Well-Lighted Place"	An old Cuban fisherman, Santiago, fallen on hard luck, hooks the largest fish of his career only to have it consumed by sharks before he can bring it to shore.
6	*A Day In the Life of Ivan Denisovitch ,* Solzhenitsyn	A Russian man struggles to retain his humanity in the face of the abuses of a Soviet concentration camp.
7	*To Kill A Mockingbird ,* Lee	Two children, Scout and Jem, become both witnesses and victims to social bigotry and racism when their father, a court appointed lawyer, defends an innocent black man accused of raping a white woman.

Conflict	Theme	Aids/Devices	Alternate Title	Class
Man vs. Society Man vs Nature	Dreams/Visions Daring	Alliteration	*So Few Of Me*, Reynolds	1
Man vs. Society Man vs. Man Man vs. Nature	Freedom vs. Tyranny, the triumph of the human spirit	Imagery	*The Three Golden Keys*, Sis	1
Man vs. Man Man vs. Society Man vs. Nature Man vs. Fate	The "Noble Savage" Heroism Loyalty Revenge	Types, symbolism, imagery	*Heart of Darkness*, Conrad	2
Man vs. Society Man vs. Self Man vs. God Man vs. Man	Consequences of adultery (sin) Effects of unconfessed sin/guilty Effects of bitterness Revenge Slavery vs. Freedom	Symbolism	*The Last of the Mohicans*, Cooper	3
Man vs. Nature Man vs. Man Man vs. Self Man vs. Society	Mechanization of man Brutality of war The importance of empathy Determinism	Symbolism, imagery, metaphor, simile	*The Open Boat,* Crane	4
Man vs. Nature Man vs. Himself Man vs. Fate	Grace under pressure Empathy Disinterestedness of nature Courage in the face of a meaningless world	Symbolism, allusion	*The Pearl,* Steinbeck or *Of Mice and Men*, Steinbeck	5
Man vs. Man Man vs. Society Man vs. Self	The indomitable human spirit Freedom vs. Tyranny Atrocity of Communism	Symbolism	*The Death of Ivan Ilyich,* Tolstoy	6
Man vs. Man Man vs. Society Man vs. Himself	Lost innocence Coming of Age Self-Sacrifical Love Racial Prejudice Source of Virtue/Honor	Symbolism, allusion, simile, metaphor	*The Call of the Wild*, London	7

Chapter 4

The Quarterly Model

The Quarterly Model

The Quarterly Model is intended for single families conducting quarterly classes in situations where literature is not the primary focus and teachers have many non-literature demands on their time. For younger students, these classes range from 90 minutes to two hours in length. For older students, plan 3 hours for discussion, taking a break midway. The book lists assume you will meet the class the first week of the year, then every 9 weeks thereafter for a total of 5 meetings in a 36 week academic year. This model lends itself to occasional teacher training seminars, SAT preparation courses, etc.

Kindergarten and First Grade:

This model may be employed in younger elementary classrooms where teachers wish to introduce students to the study of literature, but aren't yet prepared to engage them with any great regularity. This method may allow teachers to introduce literary terminology and basic story structure, both of which will suit the student for future participation in literary analysis. The seasonal model does not take the place of a formal reading class, which is imperative for student growth at this level.

Class 1 – Read a single illustrated children's story aloud to students in class. Introduce the story elements individually, noting them as they occur in the specific story in question. Introduce any literary devices that occur within the story. Plot the story on a plot chart. Follow up with a related art or craft activity or a coloring sheet.

Class 2 – Review the elements of story with the class. Read the next story book listed for the Seasonal Model within your grade level. Plot the story on the board using the plot chart diagram. Lead children in a discussion to identify theme. Notice literary devices. Use the appropriate literary vocabulary to identify basic story parts. Teach children to parrot the vocabulary. Drill them in story structure. After completing the plot chart, ask students to retell the story from the plot chart (narration). This aids in story sequencing and reading comprehension skills. Help the students summarize the story in a single sentence. Do another art extension project.

Class 3-5 – Continue to work through the titles for the seasonal list at your grade level as directed in the charts that follow.

Second through Sixth Grades:

Present the material to these students in the same manner as with their younger counterparts. However, after plotting the story and discovering the theme, ask for some work in narration and composition. Ask students to retell the story orally from their plot chart outlines. Ask them to rewrite the story in their own words from their plot charts. Advanced students may change or add details to create their own versions (for example, alter the story's setting or the characters' personalities for variety). This may turn into a creative writing exercise. Ask them to retain the basic plot line and themes in their own versions and credit the original author. More information on this exercise is available in *Teaching Writing: Structure and Style*, published by the Institute for Excellence in Writing.

Seventh through Twelfth Grades:

Older students should be expected to write about the books they discuss in class. Assign an essay after your class discussion. See chapter 5, "Writing from Literature."

Class 1 – Discussion leader teaches the method for analysis presented in the *Teaching the Classics* Basic Seminar. Books for discussion will include several children's picture story books. Instructor will guide the class to identify story elements including setting, character, conflict, plot structure, and theme. Literary devices will be identified as they occur.

Classes 2-5 – Discussion leader will guide the class to identify story elements within each novel in turn, utilizing the same method used to analyze children's books in the previous lesson. Leader will employ the Socratic method to stimulate discussion, using the Socratic List provided in the Appendix of the *Teaching the Classics* basic seminar.

The Quarterly Model is insufficient for the literature classroom whose aim is breadth of coverage and scope. This model allows for deep coverage of a few titles in an academic year.

_____

_____

_____

_____

_____

_____

_____

_____

_____

_____

_____

_____

_____

_____

Kindergarten

Class	Title	Plot
1	*The Bee Tree, Polacco*	A reluctant reader learns the sweetness of hard won success when her grandfather takes her on a bee hunt.
2	*The Tale of Peter Rabbit*, Potter	Peter disobeys his mother's order and sneaks into Mr. McGregor's garden, losing his new clothes and catching a terrible cold.
3	*Apples to Oregon*, Hopkinson	Daddy and Delicious embark on a journey from Iowa to Oregon with a "nursery" wagon full of fruit trees and hearts full of hope.
4	*The Keeping Quilt*, Polacco	An immigrant family preserves its heritage and memories in a special keepsake: a quilt that becomes a family heirloom.
5	*Peter and the Wolf*, Prokofiev	When Peter goes beyond the garden gate, he is stalked by a ravenous wolf.

Conflict	Theme	Aids/Devices	Alternate Title	Class
Man vs. Nature, Man vs. Self	Rewards of patience and perseverance, the sweetness of success	Alliteration, Dialect, Symbolism	*Why Mosquitoes Buzz in People's Ears*, Aardema	1
Man vs. Man, Man vs. Nature	Consequences of disobedience	*Teaching the Classics* basic seminar	*The Tale of Benjamin Bunny*, Potter	2
Man vs. Nature	Determination, perseverance, cooperation, vision	*Ready Readers* at CenterForLit website	*King Bidgood's In the Bathtub*, Wood	3
Man vs. Nature	The preservation of heritage and family in the face of time's passage	Symbolism	*Thank You, Mr. Falker*, Polacco	4
Man vs. Nature	Man's dominion over nature	Anthropomorphism	*The Whispering Rabbit*, Brown	5

Class	Title	Plot
1	*The Story of Ferdinand,* Leaf	Unlike the other bulls, Ferdinand refuses to fight in the bullfights in Madrid, preferring peaceful contemplation in his meadow.
2	*Brave Irene,* Steig	When her seamstress mother is taken ill, young Irene braves a snowstorm to deliver a gown commissioned by the duchess.
3	*A Bargain for Frances,* Hoban	Frances, swindled by her friend Thelma, gets even.
4	*Horton Hears a Who,* Seuss	Horton the elephant hears tiny voices on a floating dust mote and struggles to protect the tiny lives they represent in spite of his skeptical, scoffing neighbors.
5	*The Biggest Bear,* Ward	When little Johnny's pet bear cub grows to become a neghborhood nuisance, he must make a man's decision.

Conflict	Theme	Aids/Devices	Alternate Title	Class
Man vs Man, Man vs. Nature	Pacifism, individuality	Teacher Guide at CenterForLit website	*The Church Mouse,* Graham	1
Man vs. Nature, Man vs. Self	Bravery, determination, loyalty, integrity	*Ready Readers* at CenterForLit website	*The Wing Shop* , Woodruff	2
Man vs. Man	Friendship, shrewdness, coming of age	Auido Lecture at CenterForLit website	*The Fool of the World and the Flying Ship,* Ransome	3
Man vs. Society	Sanctity of life, Faith, Persecution	Rhyme	*The Stranger* , VanAllsburg	4
Man vs. Nature, Man vs. Self, Man vs. Man	Meaning of manhood, courage; Coming of Age	Pun, parody, irony, understatement	*Caps For Sale* , Slobodkina	5

Class	Title	Plot
1	*Amos and Boris, Steig*	The story of an unlikely friendship between a mouse and a whale reminiscient of Aesop's fable of the mouse and the lion.
2	*Mouse Soup* , Lobel	Shrewd Mouse invents stories to entertain Weasel and escape becoming his dinner.
3	*My Father's Dragon* , Gannet	The narrator relates the story of his clever father, Elmer Elevator, who journeys to the land of Tangerina to free a dragon who's been enslaved by the other islanders.
4	*The Bears On Hemlock Mountain* , Dagliesh	When a young boy travels over the mountain on an errand for his mother, he discovers that there **are** bears on Hemlock Mountain.
5	*The Matchlock Gun* , Edmonds	Young Edward, his mother and his little sister must protect themselves from unfriendly indians while father is away fighting with the militia.

Conflict	Theme	Aids/Devices	Alternate Title	Class
Man vs. Nature	Kindness remembered, friendship	Alliteration, Anthropomorphism	*Tops and Bottoms* , Stevens	1
Man vs. Man	Mouse proves the value of reading and thinking in this humorous tale; shrewdness.	Story frame	*The 100 Dresses* , Estes	2
Man vs. Nature, Man vs. Society	Forethought, kindness, friendship, compassion, loyalty	Alliteration	*Benjamin West and His Cat, Grimalkin,* Henry	3
Man vs. Nature, Man vs. Self	Courage and responsibility, actions and consequences	Foreshadowing, imagery, repetition	*Stuart Little,* White	4
Man vs. Man, Man vs Self	Courage, obedience, coming of age	Foreshadowing	*Billy Blaze adventures,*	5

Class	Title	Plot
1	*Dr. De Soto* , Steig	Dr. De Soto, a mouse and the town dentist, must employ not only his expertise but also his wits when he treats a wily and hungry fox who has a tooth ache.
1	*Winnie the Pooh, "The House at Pooh Corner - In Which Eeyore Finds the Wolery and Owl Moves Into It",* Milne	When Owl loses his home to a wind storm, the other residents of the 100 acre wood help him relocate.
1	*Horton Hears A Who* , Seuss	Horton's keen ears hear better than most and make him alone responsible for protecting the wee people of Who-ville from annihilation.
2	*The Cricket In Times Square* , Selden	Chester the cricket and Mario the newsboy learn the self-sacrificial nature of real friendship as they endeavor to care for one another.
3	*The Mouse and the Motorcycle,* Cleary	Ralph, a mouse who lives in a roadside inn with his family, befriends and saves the life of a young boy, who rewards him with a gift of a toy motorcycle.
4	*Misty of Chincoteague* , Henry	Paul and Maureen Bibee work hard to earn money to buy the famous Phantom and her colt at the yearly pony auction on Chincoteague Island.
5	*Charlotte's Web* , White	When Fern's petted piglet Wilbur moves to the barn, his loneliness and fears are abated by his friendship with Charlotte, a sagacious grey barn spider.

Conflict	Theme	Aids/Devices	Alternate Title	Class
Man vs. Man	Courage, ethics, consequences. The triumph of good vs. evil. "He who lays a trap for another, his own feet will find it."	Anthropomorphism, Irony	*Ben and Me,* Lawson	1
Man vs. Nature Man vs. Man Man vs. Self	Self-sacrificial love and friendship	Personification	*Pippi Longstocking*, Lindgren	1
Man vs. Man Man vs. Society	Self-Sacrifice, Mob violence, the Value of life ("A person's a person no matter how small!")	Rhyme	*The Boxcar Children*, Warner	1
Man vs. Nature Man vs. Self	The nature of friendship; the importance of freedom	*Ready Readers* at CenterForLit website	*Henry and Ribsy*, Cleary	2
Man vs. Nature Man vs. Man Man vs. Self	Personal responsibility, courage, friendship	Alliteration, assonance, onomatopoeia, anthropomorphism	*Homer Price*, McCloskey	3
Man vs. Nature Man vs. Self Man vs. Man	Stewardship/Dominion Mandate; Selfishness vs Selflessness; Sacrificial love; Coming of Age	*Ready Readers* at CenterForLit website	*The Great Brain*, Fitzgerald	4
Man vs. Nature Man vs. Self Man vs. Man	Self- Sacrificial love and friendship: "Greater love has no man than this, that he would lay down his life for a friend."	Anthropomorphism	*A Little Princess*, Burnett	5

4th Grade

Class	Title	Plot
1	*Lentil,* McCloskey	For Lentil, a young boy whose singing voice is a bit below par, playing the harmonica is just the thing; his town thinks so too when he saves the day with his talent.
1	*Bedtime For Frances,* Hoban	Frances, a badger, hates bedtime and does her best to delay it.
1	*Apples To Oregon,* Hopkinson	Delicious and her daddy are determined to move their family and their orchard to the temperate state of Oregon.
2	*Wind In the Willows,* Grahame	Fickle Mr. Toad of Toad Hall becomes entranced by the faddish new motorcar; his friends endeavor to recall him to his senses and restore to him his dignity and place in the community.
3	*Charlie and the Chocolate Factory,* Dahl	When Charlie Bucket discovers a golden ticket in his Wonka Bar, he embarks on an adventure that tests his character and reveals his personal integrity.
4	*Trumpet of the Swan,* White	Louis, a swan born mute, learns to communicate by means of a trumpet that his father steals from a local music store; with the trumpet, he earns enough money to repay his father's debt to the store owner.
5	*Miracle On Maple Hill,* Sorenson	A young girl and her family return to her mother's childhood home on Maple Hill in search of rest and respite for their father, a recovered POW.

Conflict	Theme	Aids/Devices	Alternate Title	Class
Man vs. Self Man vs. Man	Cheerfulness, diligence, value of the individual	Onomatopoeia	*How the Grinch Stole Christmas*, Seuss	1
Man vs. Man Man vs. Self	Obedience, consequences	Rhyme, onomatopoeia	*Roxaboxen,* Cohen	1
Man vs. Nature Man vs. Society Man vs. Self	Determination, Cooperation, Vision, Westward Expansion, the Pioneer Spirit, Industry	*Ready Readers* at CenterForLit website	*Stellaluna,* Canon	1
Man vs. Man Man vs. Society Man vs. Self	City vs. Country, Industrialization, Urbanization, Value of community, Social Hierarchy, True Friendship	Classics Club DVD at CenterforLit website	*Owls In the Family*, Mowat	2
Man vs. Society Man vs. Self Man vs. Man	Value of personal integrity, Honesty, Deception	Rhyme, symbolism	*The Penderwicks,* Birdsall	3
Man vs. Man Man vs. Self Man vs. Nature	Character qualities such as determination, integrity, commitment, ethics; remuneration; fatherly love	*Ready Readers* at CenterForLit website	*Swiss Family Robinson*, Wyss	4
Man vs. Society Man vs. Self Man vs. Nature	Regeneration/Renewal, Value of Community, Coming of Age/Growing Up	*Ready Readers* at CenterForLit website	*Five Children and It*, Nesbit	5

Class	Title	Plot
1	*Why Mosquitoes Buzz In People's Ears,* Aardema	In this African fable, a mosquito's foolishness touches off an unexpected, tragic chain of events.
1	*Chrysanthemum,* Henkes	Chrysanthemum overcomes peer teasing and learns to love her name.
1	*TheBee Tree* , Polacco	A girl, tired of struggling with books, goes with her grandfather on a bee tree hunt and learns to savor the sweet rewards of hard won success.
2	*A Door In the Wall* , DeAngeli	Robin, a young nobleman's son, is struck with paralysis and abandoned by his household; a monk nurses him to health and teaches him self-discipline, industry, and respect for others.
3	Shakespeare Intro using Lamb's Tales, "Macbeth" and the original play *Macbeth,* Shakespeare	When noble Macbeth, tempted by evil spirits, murders his kinsman and king, he finds he may keep his ill-gotten crown only through further bloodshed.
4	*Straw Into Gold,* Schmidt	Drawing on the timeless fairytale of *Rumplestiltskin,* this story provides a reason for the little man's seemingly capricious act.
5	*The Chronicles of Narnia* , Lewis	The Pevensie children stumble into another land by way of an enchanted wardrobe and come to know not only themselves, but also the Lord of the land, Aslan, and the nature of love.

5th Grade

Quarterly Model

Conflict	Theme	Aids/Devices	Alternate Title	Class
Man vs. Man Man vs. Himself	Actions have consequences.	Onomatopoeia	*The Apple and the Arrow*, Buff	1
Man vs. Man Man vs. Himself	Self-confidence, Fear of Man, Peer problems, envy/jealousy	Pun	*King Arthur The Sword in the Stone*, Talbott	1
Man vs. Nature Man vs. Himself	Sweetness of hard won success, perseverance, rewards of diligence	Alliteration, Dialect, Rhyme, Symbolism	*When I Was Young in the Mountains*, Rylant	1
Man vs. God Man vs. Self Man vs. Nature Man vs. Society	Goodness and character are born through suffering. Providence. Grace	*Ready Readers* at CenterForLit website	*From the Mixed Up Files of Mrs. Basil E. Frankweiler*, Konigsburg	2
Man vs. Self Man vs. Society Man vs. Man Man vs. Fate	Sin Nature (Fatal Flaw), Deceitfulness of the human heart, Dangers of selfish ambition	Poetic devices, blank verse, pun, double entendre	*The Invention of Hugo Cabret*, Selznick	3
Man vs. Man Man vs. Society Man vs. Self Man vs. Providence	Selfless Love, Comparison and discussion of strength and weakness, Providence, Appearance vs. Reality	Frame, Imagery, Foreshadowing, Sensory Language	*Soup,* Robert Newton Peck	4
Man vs. Man Man vs. Self Man vs. Society Man vs. God	Sin Nature of Man, Sacrificial Love and Substitutionary Atonement, Redemption, the effects of Envy, Betrayal	Frame, Symbolism, Anthropomorphism	*Voyage of the Dawn Treader*, Lewis	5

Class	Title	Plot
1	*The Gardener*, Stewart	Lydia Grace must leave her family and live with her uncle in the city during the depression; her cheerful countenance and graciousness make her a blessing to everyone around her.
1	*Paul Revere's Ride,* Longfellow	The great American Poet Laureate tells the story of Paul Revere's famous ride to alert the Minutemen of the British soldiers' approach on the eve of the battle of Lexington & Concord in 1775.
1	*Crossing Bok Chitto,* Tingle	The friendship between an African American slave child and a Native American child facilitates a slave escape.
2	*Tuck Everlasting,* Babbitt	A young girl befriends the Tuck family, who have accidentally discovered the fountain of youth. She must decide whether to live a natural life herself and how to help them keep their secret from those who would exploit it.
3	*Julius Caesar,* Shakespeare	Brutus, Cassius and the other conspirators plot and perform the assassination of Julius Caesar. They then fight with the Triumvirate for control of Rome, only to find that the ambitious spirit for which they killed Caesar dwells in their own hearts as well.
4	*At the Back of the North Wind,* MacDonald	A sickly boy journeys with the mythical North Wind to faraway lands and learns of her trustworthiness, faithfulness and love.
5	*Treasure Island,* Stevenson	Jim Hawkins, whose family is deeply in debt, discovers a pirate's treasure map and embarks on a dangerous journey to find the treasure, encountering honest men and ruffians in equal measure along the way.

Conflict	Theme	Aids/Devices	Alternate Title	Class
Man vs. Society Man vs. Man Man vs. Self	Bloom where you are planted A cheerful heart does good like a medicine	Teacher Guide at CenterForLit website	*The Friend*, Stewart	1
Man v. Man Man v. Society	Patriotism Liberty	*Teaching the Classics* basic seminar	*The Old Woman Who Named Things*, Rylant	1
Man v. Man Man v. Society	Friendship across racial boundaries; the incongruity of slavery	Teacher Guide at CenterForLit website	*Grandfather's Journey*, Say	1
Man v. Nature Man v. Man Man v. Self	The story explores the natural order of things and the consequences of upsetting this order.	Symbolism, Imagery	*Anne of Green Gables*, Montgomery	2
Man v. Man Man v. Self Man v. Society	The wickedness of the human heart The law of sowing and reaping Tyranny Ambition Frailty	*Ready Readers* at CenterForLit website	*Mrs. Frisbee & the Rats of NIMH*, O'Brien	3
Man v. God Man v. Man	This allegory explores the problem of pain and the nature of death while depicting goodness, kindness and charity.	*Ready Readers* at CenterForLit website	*A Girl of the Limberlost*, Porter	4
Man v. Man Man v. Self	Coming of Age Shrewdness/Resourcefulness Honesty Mercy Friendship	*Ready Readers* at CenterForLit website	*The Pushcart War*, Merrill	5

Class	Title	Plot
1	*The Keeping Quilt,* Polacco	A Russian immigrant makes an heirloom quilt for her daughter out of the rag clothing of family members she's left behind.
1	*Amos & Boris,* Steig	When the mouse Amos's ship capsizes, he is rescued by the whale Boris; years later, Amos returns the favor unexpectedly.
1	*A Bargain for Frances,* Hoban	When Frances's friend Thelma takes advantage of her, Frances finds a way to get even.
2	*The Bronze Bow*, Speare	Daniel bar-Jamin, a rugged runaway who has cast his lot with the zealots, is recalled to responsibility by his grandmother's death. He must wrestle with his hatred for the Romans who occupy Israel and his growing love for his people.
3	*The Odyssey,* Homer	Odysseus, who has struggled 10 years in the Trojan war and been delayed from homecoming another 10 years for offending the gods, finally regains his home.
4	*Huckleberry Finn,* Twain	Vagabond Huck and runaway slave Jim try to escape society by floating down the Mississippi River on a raft.
5	*Great Expectations*, Dickens	When the impoverished orphan Pip discovers that he has come into an inheritance from a mysterious benefactor, he distances himself from his humble friends and family to better himself and earn the love of the wealthy and beautiful Estella.

7th Grade

Conflict	Theme	Aids/Devices	*Alternate Title*	Class
Man v. Nature	The value of family heritage	Symbolism	*The Fool of the World and the Flying Ship,* Ransome	1
Man v. Nature	Friendship Kindness Faithfulness & Loyalty	Descriptive language	*Casey At the Bat,* retold by Polacco	1
Man v. Man Man v. Self	Deception Shrewdness Friendship Coming of Age	Audio Lecture at CenterForLit website	*Thunder Cake,* Polacco	1
Man v. Society Man v. Self Man v. God	Bitterness & its Effects The nature of forgiveness Sacrificial love Redemption	*Ready Readers* at CenterForLit website	*The Devil's Arithmetic,* Yolen	2
Man v. gods Man v. Man	The importance of marriage and family Faithfulness Patriotism and loyalty Justice	Epic Simile	*The Wanderings of Odysseus,* Sutcliffe (a re-telling of The Odyssey for young readers)	3
Man v. Sociey Man v. Man Man v. Self	Freedom & Slavery Character & Integrity Racism Pride vs. Humility Social Conventions	Classics Club DVD at CenterForLit website	*Henry V,* Shakespeare	4
Man v. Self Man v. Man Man vs. Society	Redemptive Love Pride vs. Humility Appearance vs. Reality Fear of Man; Bitterness Coming of Age; Friendship	Symbolism, imagery, allegory, foreshadowing	*Kidnapped,* Stevenson	5

Class	Title	Plot
1	*I Have an Olive Tree,* Bunting	7 year old Greek immigrant Sophie wants a skateboard for her birthday; instead, Grandpa gives her an olive tree in their homeland.
1	*The Biggest Bear,* Ward	A young boy must rid the neighborhood of his beloved pet bear, who has become a nuisance.
1	*Letting Swift River Go,* Yolen	Visiting the inundated Swift River Valley which once was her home, Sally Jane makes peace with her drowned past.
2	*The Iliad,* Homer	Greek warrior and demi-god Achilles, embittered by King Agamemnon's ill treatment, refuses to reconcile and withdraws from the battle between the Greeks and the Trojans.
3	*The Yearling,* Rawlings	Jody must give up his childhood and embrace the responsibilities of a man when his pet fawn grows up to menace the family farm.
4	*A Tale of Two Cities,* Dickens	Exiled aristocrat Charles Darnay returns to France during the Reign of Terror; without the aid of family friend Sydney Carton, he will be executed, leaving his family desolate.
5	*The Hobbit,* Tolkien	Homebody Bilbo Baggins is petitioned by the wizard Gandalf to accompany a group of dwarves on a mission to burgle stolen treasure from the evil dragon Smaug.

Conflict	Theme	Aids/Devices	Alternate Title	Class
Man vs. Man	Heritage Maturity	Symbolism	*Eleanor,* Cooney	1
Man v. Nature Man v. Self Man v. Society	Manhood/Masculinity What is courage? Self-denial What is strength?	Pun, parody, irony, understatement	*Mirette On the High Wire,* McCulley	1
Man v. Society Man v. Nature Man v. Self	The nature of time Bitterness & forgiveness Link between acceptance & peace	*Ready Readers* at CenterForLit website	*Angelo,* Macaulay	1
Man v. Man Man v. Self Man v. gods	Bitterness & its consequences Honor Pride Loyalty & Friendship	Epic Simile, *In Medias Res*	*Black Ships Before Troy,* Sutcliffe (a re-telling of the Iliad for children)	2
Man v. Nature Man v. Man Man v. Self	Coming of Age Childhood v. Manhood	Classics Club DVD at CenterForLit website	*A Connecticut Yankee in King Arthur's Court,* Twain	3
Man v. Society Man v. Man Man v. Self	Sacrificial Love Bitterness & Revenge Faithfulness & Devotion Tyranny & Liberty	Teacher Guide at CenterForLit website	*A Wrinkle in Time,* L'Engle	4
Man v. Self Man v. Man Man v. Society	Greed vs. Contentment Faithfulness, Selflessness Appearances v. Realities Strength coming from Weakness Good v. Evil	*Ready Readers* at CenterForLit website	*The House of 60 Fathers,* Meindert de Jong	5

9th Grade

Class	Title	Plot
1	*Fishing In the Air*, Creech	A boy and his father go on a fishing trip and catch more than they expect.
1	*Owl Moon,* Yolen	A child experiences a family rite of passage when he goes owling with his father.
1	*All the Places to Love,* MacLachlan	A boy remembers all the places he's come to love and the people with whom they're associated, promising to share them with his new baby sister.
2	*The Aeneid*, Virgil	Aeneas flees a burning Troy and journeys with other refugees to establish a new homeland on the coast of Italy.
3	*Romeo and Juliet,* Shakespeare	Impetuous teen lovers from feuding families forsake their parents' authority when they marry secretly; disaster ensues.
4	*Frankenstein,* Shelley	Scientific genius Victor Frankenstein seeks immortality by creating life. His creature does not meet expectations. The disastrous consequences that follow force us to face questions about the nature of man, God and Nature.
5	*The Strange Case of Dr. Jekyll and Mr. Hyde,* Stevenson	A narrator discovers that the respectable doctor he has long called his friend is also the mysterious menace who has committed a string of heinous crimes in late 19th century London.

Conflict	Theme	Aids/Devices	Alternate Title	Class
Man vs. Nature Man vs. Self	Family Heritage, the Nature of Time, Memory	*Ready Readers* at CenterForLit website	*Don Quixote,* Williams	1
Man vs. Nature Man vs. Self	Self-control, Patience, Coming of Age	Imagery, Simile, Metaphor	*Sir Gawain and the Green Knight,* Morpurgo	1
Man vs. Nature	Generational heritage, the value of the land, mortality	*Ready Readers* at CenterForLit website	*Albert,* Napoli	1
Man v. Society Man v. Man Man v. the gods	Providence Patriotism - superiority of national to personal vision	Epic simile, alliteration, personification, allegory, irony	*The Prince and the Pauper,* Twain	2
Man v. Man Man v. God	Consequences of bitterness, and rashness Consequences of rebellion Dangers of deception Star crossed love	Poetic devices: blank verse, pun, irony, etc.	*Merchant of Venice,* Shakespeare	3
Man v. Nature Man v. God Man v. Man	What is a human being? Creature/Creator distinction	Flashback	*Good Morning, Miss Dove,* Patton	4
Man v. Man Man v. Self Man v. God Man v. Nature	Human Nature Original Sin Role of the Conscience Pride & Ambition	Foreshadowing	*The Black Falcon,* Sperry	5

Class	Title	Plot
1	*Beowulf,* picture storybook	Beowulf the Geat, hero of his people, voyages to the land of king Hrothgar, to whom he owes a family debt. There he delivers Hrothgar's people from the monster scourge Grendel.
1	*Canterbury Tales,* retold by Barbara Cohen	An introduction to the famous tales of Geoffrey Chaucer, this book includes short re-tellings of the Nun's Priest's Tale, the Pardoner's Tale, the Wife of Bath's Tale and the Franklin's Tale.
1	*The Clown of God,* DePaola	An orphan boy discovers his talent for juggling and makes a place for himself in society. When old age eventually robs him of it, he finds he still has place with God.
2	*Beowulf*	Beowulf the Geat, hero of his people, voyages to the land of king Hrothgar, to whom he owes a family debt. There he delivers Hrothgar's people from the monster scourge Grendel.
3	*Divine Comedy: The Inferno,* Dante	Genre: Epic Poetry. In his middle age, the narrator, aided by the beautiful Beatrice and guided by the wise poet Virgil, travels through hell to understand the nature, breadth and consequences of sin.
4	*Canterbury Tales,* Chaucer (selections: General Prologue, Nun's Priest's Tale, Pardoner's Tale, Knight's Tale)	A diverse group of 14th century English men and women meet on a pilgrimage to the cathedral at Canterbury. They decide to pass time along the journey with a storytelling contest.
5	*The Great Divorce,* Lewis	A day trip to the outer regions of Heaven gives inhabitants of Hell a once-in-a-lifetime opportunity: to experience paradise and its "Solid People" and choose their own citizenship.

Conflict	Theme	Aids/Devices	Alternate Title	Class
Man v. Animal/Monster, Man vs. Fate	Honor Good triumphs over evil The strength of virtue Fate	Kennings	*The Sign Painter,* Say	1
Conflicts vary, but all include Man v. Self, Man v. God	Human Nature Dangers of Pride, Greed Forgiving Debts	Allusion, irony, parody, allegory	*Chanticleer and the Fox,* Cooney	1
Man v. Society Man v. Self Man v. Nature Man v. God	Value of human life The holiness of all callings The joy of service	*Ready Readers* at CenterForLit website	*Yellow and Pink,* Steig	1
Man v. Animal/Monster, Man vs. Fate	Honor Good triumphs over evil The strength of virtue	Kennings	*Dream of the Rood* or Caedmon's *Hymn*	2
Man v. Self Man v. Man Man v. God	Fallen human nature Retributive Justice	Meter, epic simile, allegory, symbolism, allusion	*The Banquet,* Dante or *The Secret,* Petrarch	3
Every type of conflict is fully explored in this masterpiece	Human nature and its foibles The dangers of various character flaws Good triumphs over evil	Understatement, allegory, fable, irony	*Everyman,* Anonymous Medieval Drama	4
Man v. Self Man v. God	Bitterness, salvation Vanity, vice Deception Pride	Teacher Guide at CenterForLit website	*Till We Have Faces,* Lewis or *The Screwtape Letters,* Lewis	5

Class	Title	Plot
1	*The Giving Tree,* Silverstein	A chronicle of the lifelong friendship between a boy and a tree.
1	**Wilfrid Gordon Macdonald Partridge,** Fox	Wilfrid, a small boy, helps Miss Nancy, his elderly frend, find her memory.
1	*The Spider and the Fly* , DiTerlizzi	A flattering spider entices a gullible fly into his parlor.
2	*Paradise Lost* , Milton	The fallen angel, Lucifer, seeks revenge upon the Creator God by conducting a sneak attack on His newest creation, man.
3	*Hamlet,* Shakespeare	The noble prince of Denmark decides to avenge his father's murder, but struggles to make good on his pledge.
4	*Bleak House* , Dickens	Orphan Esther Summerson seeks friendship and belonging among a family of Chancery suitors, while the noble Lady Dedlock struggles to protect a horrible secret.
5	*Wuthering Heights* , Bronte	A traveler uncovers the secret past of a wild and violent landowner, Heathcliff, and his one time beloved Kathy.

Conflict	Theme	Aids/Devices	Alternate Title	Class
Man vs. Man	Self-sacrificial love	Personification	*Always Room For One More*, Leodhas	1
Man vs. Nature Man vs. Self	The universal human experience The nature of friendship	*Ready Readers* at CenterForLit website	*The Tale of Meshka the Kvetch*, Chapman	1
Man vs. Man Man vs. Self	Dangers of flattery/pride	Anthropomorphism	*Song of the Swallows*, Politi	1
Creature vs. Creator, Man vs. man	The Fall of Man Origins of Sin	Epic Simile, Epic devices	*Lycidas,* Milton	2
Man vs. Himself Man vs. Fate Man vs. Man	Human frailty The Tragic Hero Sanity vs. Insanity Revenge	Classics Club DVD at CenterForLit website	*Henry V,* Shakespeare	3
Man vs. Society Man vs. Man	Justice	Simile, personification, imagery	*David Copperfield*, Dickens	4
Man vs. Man Man vs. Society	Perverse love/Selfish love The nature of passion Revenge/Bitterness/Betrayal Manipulation Social Prejudice	Gothic Romance, symbolism, imagery	*The Dubliners*, Joyce	5

Class	Title	Plot
1	*Emily,* Bedard	A curious child chronicles her relationship with her introverted neighbor, the poet Emily Dickinson.
1	*The Man Who Walked Between the Towers,* Gerstein	True life narrative of the French tightrope artist who walked a wire strung between the historic twin towers.
1	*The Wall,* Sis	A Czechoslovakian boy grows up in a communist state.
2	*Last of the Mohicans* , Cooper	English soliders, American scouts and Mohican and Huron warriors engage in battle, intrigue and romance during the 18th century French and Indian War.
3	*The Red Badge of Courage* , Crane	Young and naïve Henry joins the Union Army with visions of valour and heroism, but finds such valor impossible in a world without universal truth and meaning.
4	Hemingway Unit: *The Old Man and the Sea,* "Today Is Friday," "A Clean, Well-Lighted Place"	An old Cuban fisherman, Santiago, fallen on hard luck, hooks the largest fish of his career only to have it consumed by sharks before he can bring it to shore.
5	*To Kill A Mockingbird* , Lee	Two children, Scout and Jem, become both witnesses and victims to social bigotry and racism when their father, a court appointed lawyer, defends an innocent black man accused of raping a white woman.

Conflict	Theme	Aids/Devices	Alternate Title	Class
Man vs. Society	Reclusiveness/Shyness Quiet Joy Friendship	Rhythm, metaphor, alliteration, simile, personification	*My Uncle Emily, Yolen*	1
Man vs. Society Man vs Nature	Dreams/Visions Daring	Alliteration	*So Few Of Me*, Reynolds	1
Man vs. Society Man vs. Man Man vs. Nature	Freedom vs. Tyranny, the triumph of the human spirit	Imagery	*The Three Golden Keys*, Sis	1
Man vs. Man Man vs. Society Man vs. Nature Man vs. Fate	The "Noble Savage" Heroism Loyalty Revenge	Types, symbolism, imagery	*Heart of Darkness*, Conrad	2
Man vs. Nature Man vs. Man Man vs. Self Man vs. Society	Mechanization of man Brutality of war The importance of empathy Determinism	Symbolism, imagery, metaphor, simile	*The Open Boat,* Crane	3
Man vs. Nature Man vs. Himself Man vs. Fate	Grace under pressure Empathy Disinterestedness of nature Courage in the face of a meaningless world	Symbolism, allusion	*The Pearl,* Steinbeck or *Of Mice and Men*, Steinbeck	4
Man vs. Man Man vs. Society Man vs. Himself	Lost innocence Coming of Age Self-Sacrifical Love Racial Prejudice Source of Virtue/Honor	Symbolism, allusion, simile, metaphor	*The Call of the Wild*, London	5

Chapter 5

The Seasonal Model

The Seasonal Model

Like the Quarterly Model, the Seasonal Model is intended for single families conducting seasonal classes where literature is not the primary focus and teachers have many non-literature demands on their time. This model also lends itself to occasional teacher training seminars, SAT preparation courses, etc.

Students in grades K-3 will use 90 minutes to 2 hours for a class discussion. Older students will use more time, with high school students requiring up to 3 hours for a discussion session.

A model for seasonal instruction follows:

Kindergarten and First Grade:

This model may be employed in younger elementary classrooms where teachers wish to introduce students to the study of literature, but aren't yet prepared to engage them with any great regularity. This method may allow teachers to introduce literary terminology and basic story structure, both of which will suit the student for future participation in literary analysis. The seasonal model does not take the place of a formal reading class, which is imperative for student growth at this level.

Class 1 – Read a single illustrated children's story aloud to students in class. Introduce the story elements individually, noting them as they occur in the specific story in question. Introduce any literary devices that occur within the story.

Class 2 – Review the elements of story with the class. Read the next story book listed for the Seasonal Model within your grade level. Plot the story on the board using the plot chart diagram. Lead children in a discussion to identify theme. Notice literary devices. Use the appropriate literary vocabulary to identify basic story parts. Teach children to parrot the vocabulary. Drill them in story structure. After completing the plot chart, ask students to retell the story from the plot chart (narration). This aids in story sequencing and reading comprehension skills. Help the students summarize the story in a single sentence.

Class 3-4 – Continue to work through the titles for the seasonal list at your grade level as directed in the charts below.

Second through Sixth Grades:

Class 1 – Discussion leader teaches the method for analysis presented in the *Teaching the Classics* Basic Seminar. Books for discussion will include several children's picture story books. Instructor will guide the class to identify story elements including setting, character, conflict, plot structure, and theme. Literary devices will be identified as they occur.

Classes 2-4 – Discussion leader will guide the class to identify story elements within each novel, utilizing the same method used in the previous lesson with children's. Teacher will employ the

Socratic method to stimulate discussion, using the Socratic List provided in the appendix of the *Teaching the Classics* basic seminar.

Add a narrative component with students at this level. Ask them to retell the story orally from the plot chart outline. Once they have verbalized the plot, have them re-write the story in their own words, crediting the author for the original, of course.

Seventh through Twelfth Grades:

7th through 12th graders will complete 3 children's books and 3 grade level titles by the year's end.

Class 1 – Read the picture books in turn, identifying the individual elements of story and plotting each on a plot chart in order to arrive at a discussion of theme. By the time students at this level have practiced with 3 story books, they should be ready to discuss books at their own reading level.

Class 2 – Discuss the first grade level selection. Students should come to class having read the story in full. Plot the story, identifying structural elements. Discuss thematic implications. Be sure to address issues of context, encouraging students to build their lit notebooks sections regarding literary eras and biographical information on authors.

Classes 3 and 4 – Follow the same method to complete the reading list.

In addition to identifying the elements listed above, older students should be expected to write about the books they discuss in class. Assign an essay after your class discussion. See chapter 5, "Writing from Literature."

The Seasonal Model is insufficient for the literature classroom whose aim is breadth of coverage and scope. This model allows for deep coverage of a few titles in an academic year.

_____

_____

_____

_____

_____

_____

_____

_____

Class	Title	Plot
1	*The Tale of Peter Rabbit*, Potter	Peter disobeys his mother's order and sneaks into Mr. McGregor's garden, losing his new clothes and catching a terrible cold.
2	*Apples to Oregon*, Hopkinson	Daddy and Delicious embark on a journey from Iowa to Oregon with a "nursery" wagon full of fruit trees and hearts full of hope.
3	*The Keeping Quilt*, Polacco	An immigrant family preserves its heritage and memories in a special keepsake: a quilt that becomes a family heirloom.
4	*Peter and the Wolf*, Prokofiev	When Peter goes beyond the garden gate, he is stalked by a ravenous wolf.

Conflict	Theme	Aids/Devices	Alternate Title	Class
Man vs. Man, Man vs. Nature	Consequences of disobedience	*Teaching the Classics* basic seminar	*The Tale of Benjamin Bunny*, Potter	1
Man vs. Nature	Determination, perseverance, cooperation, vision	*Ready Readers* at CenterForLit website	*King Bidgood's In the Bathtub*, Wood	2
Man vs. Nature	The preservation of heritage and family in the face of time's passage	Symbolism	*Thank You, Mr. Falker*, Polacco	3
Man vs. Nature	Man's dominion over nature	Anthropomorphism	*The Whispering Rabbit*, Brown	4

1st **Grade**

Class	Title	Plot
1	*The Story of Ferdinand,* Leaf	Unlike the other bulls, Ferdinand refuses to fight in the bullfights in Madrid, preferring peaceful contemplation in his meadow.
2	*Brave Irene,* Steig	When her seamstress mother is taken ill, young Irene braves a snowstorm to deliver a gown commissioned by the duchess.
3	*A Bargain for Frances,* Hoban	Frances, swindled by her friend Thelma, gets even.
4	*The Biggest Bear,* Ward	When little Johnny's pet bear cub grows to become a neghborhood nuisance, he must make a man's decision.

Conflict	Theme	Aids/Devices	Alternate Title	Class
Man vs Man, Man vs. Nature	Pacifism, individuality	Teacher Guide at CenterForLit website	*The Church Mouse,* Graham	1
Man vs. Nature, Man vs. Self	Bravery, determination, loyalty, integrity	*Ready Readers* at CenterForLit website	*The Wing Shop* , Woodruff	2
Man vs. Man	Friendship, shrewdness, coming of age	Auido Lecture at CenterForLit website	*The Fool of the World and the Flying Ship,* Ransome	3
Man vs. Nature, Man vs. Self, Man vs. Man	Meaning of manhood, courage; Coming of Age	Pun, parody, irony, understatement	*Caps For Sale* , Slobodkina	4

Class	Title	Plot
1	*Amos and Boris, Steig*	The story of an unlikely friendship between a mouse and a whale reminiscient of Aesop's fable of the mouse and the lion.
2	*My Father's Dragon*, Gannet	The narrator relates the story of his clever father, Elmer Elevator, who journeys to the land of Tangerina to free a dragon who's been enslaved by the other islanders.
3	*The Bears On Hemlock Mountain*, Dagliesh	When a young boy travels over the mountain on an errand for his mother, he discovers that there **are** bears on Hemlock Mountain.
4	*The Matchlock Gun*, Edmonds	Young Edward, his mother and his little sister must protect themselves from unfriendly indians while father is away fighting with the militia.

Conflict	Theme	Aids/Devices	Alternate Title	Class
Man vs. Nature	Kindness remembered, friendship	Alliteration, Anthropomorphism	*Tops and Bottoms*, Stevens	1
Man vs. Nature, Man vs. Society	Forethought, kindness, friendship, compassion, loyalty	Alliteration	*Benjamin West and His Cat, Grimalkin,* Henry	2
Man vs. Nature, Man vs. Self	Courage and responsibility, actions and consequences	Foreshadowing, imagery, repetition	*Stuart Little,* White	3
Man vs. Man, Man vs Self	Courage, obedience, coming of age	Foreshadowing	*Billy Blaze adventures,*	4

Class	Title	Plot
1	*Dr. De Soto* , Steig	Dr. De Soto, a mouse and the town dentist, must employ not only his expertise but also his wits when he treats a wily and hungry fox who has a tooth ache.
1	*Winnie the Pooh, "The House at Pooh Corner - In Which Eeyore Finds the Wolery and Owl Moves Into It",* Milne	When Owl loses his home to a wind storm, the other residents of the 100 acre wood help him relocate.
1	*Horton Hears A Who* , Seuss	Horton's keen ears hear better than most and make him alone responsible for protecting the wee people of Who-ville from annihilation.
2	*The Cricket In Times Square* , Selden	Chester the cricket and Mario the newsboy learn the self-sacrificial nature of real friendship as they endeavor to care for one another.
3	*Misty of Chincoteague* , Henry	Paul and Maureen Bibee work hard to earn money to buy the famous Phantom and her colt at the yearly pony auction on Chincoteague Island.
4	*Charlotte's Web* , White	When Fern's petted piglet Wilbur moves to the barn, his loneliness and fears are abated by his friendship with Charlotte, a sagacious grey barn spider.

3rd Grade

Seasonal Model

Conflict	Theme	Aids/Devices	Alternate Title	Class
Man vs. Man	Courage, ethics, consequences. The triumph of good vs. evil. "He who lays a trap for another, his own feet will find it."	Anthropomorphism, Irony	*Ben and Me,* Lawson	1
Man vs. Nature Man vs. Man Man vs. Self	Self-sacrificial love and friendship	Personification	*Pippi Longstocking*, Lindgren	1
Man vs. Man Man vs. Society	Self-Sacrifice, Mob violence, the Value of life ("A person's a person no matter how small!")	Rhyme	*The Boxcar Children*, Warner	1
Man vs. Nature Man vs. Self	The nature of friendship; the importance of freedom	*Ready Readers* at CenterForLit website	*Henry and Ribsy*, Cleary	2
Man vs. Nature Man vs. Self Man vs. Man	Stewardship/Dominion Mandate; Selfishness vs Selflessness; Sacrificial love; Coming of Age	*Ready Readers* at CenterForLit website	*The Great Brain*, Fitzgerald	3
Man vs. Nature Man vs. Self Man vs. Man	Self- Sacrificial love and friendship: "Greater love has no man than this, that he would lay down his life for a friend."	Anthropomorphism	*A Little Princess*, Burnett	4

Reading Roadmaps: A Literary Scope & Sequence for K-12 **153**

4th Grade

Class	Title	Plot
1	*Lentil,* McCloskey	For Lentil, a young boy whose singing voice is a bit below par, playing the harmonica is just the thing; his town thinks so too when he saves the day with his talent.
1	*Bedtime For Frances,* Hoban	Frances, a badger, hates bedtime and does her best to delay it.
1	*Apples To Oregon,* Hopkinson	Delicious and her daddy are determined to move their family and their orchard to the temperate state of Oregon.
2	*Wind In the Willows,* Grahame	Fickle Mr. Toad of Toad Hall becomes entranced by the faddish new motorcar; his friends endeavor to recall him to his senses and restore to him his dignity and place in the community.
3	*Trumpet of the Swan,* White	Louis, a swan born mute, learns to communicate by means of a trumpet that his father steals from a local music store; with the trumpet, he earns enough money to repay his father's debt to the store owner.
4	*Miracle On Maple Hill*, Sorenson	A young girl and her family return to her mother's childhood home on Maple Hill in search of rest and respite for their father, a recovered POW.

Conflict	Theme	Aids/Devices	Alternate Title	Class
Man vs. Self Man vs. Man	Cheerfulness, diligence, value of the individual	Onomatopoeia	*How the Grinch Stole Christmas*, Seuss	1
Man vs. Man Man vs. Self	Obedience, consequences	Rhyme, onomatopoeia	*Roxaboxen,* Cohen	1
Man vs. Nature Man vs. Society Man vs. Self	Determination, Cooperation, Vision, Westward Expansion, the Pioneer Spirit, Industry	*Ready Readers* at CenterForLit website	*Stellaluna,* Canon	1
Man vs. Man Man vs. Society Man vs. Self	City vs. Country, Industrialization, Urbanization, Value of community, Social Hierarchy, True Friendship	Classics Club DVD at CenterforLit website	*Owls In the Family*, Mowat	2
Man vs. Man Man vs. Self Man vs. Nature	Character qualities such as determination, integrity, commitment, ethics; remuneration; fatherly love	*Ready Readers* at CenterForLit website	*Swiss Family Robinson*, Wyss	3
Man vs. Society Man vs. Self Man vs. Nature	Regeneration/Renewal, Value of Community, Coming of Age/Growing Up	*Ready Readers* at CenterForLit website	*Five Children and It*, Nesbit	4

5th Grade

Class	Title	Plot
1	*Why Mosquitoes Buzz In People's Ears,* Aardema	In this African fable, a mosquito's foolishness touches off an unexpected, tragic chain of events.
1	*Chrysanthemum,* Henkes	Chrysanthemum overcomes peer teasing and learns to love her name.
1	*TheBee Tree* , Polacco	A girl, tired of struggling with books, goes with her grandfather on a bee tree hunt and learns to savor the sweet rewards of hard won success.
2	*A Door In the Wall* , DeAngeli	Robin, a young nobleman's son, is struck with paralysis and abandoned by his household; a monk nurses him to health and teaches him self-discipline, industry, and respect for others.
3	*Straw Into Gold,* Schmidt	Drawing on the timeless fairytale of *Rumplestiltskin,* this story provides a reason for the little man's seemingly capricious act.
4	*The Chronicles of Narnia* , Lewis	The Pevensie children stumble into another land by way of an enchanted wardrobe and come to know not only themselves, but also the Lord of the land, Aslan, and the nature of love.

Conflict	Theme	Aids/Devices	Alternate Title	Class
Man vs. Man Man vs. Himself	Actions have consequences.	Onomatopoeia	*The Apple and the Arrow*, Buff	1
Man vs. Man Man vs. Himself	Self-confidence, Fear of Man, Peer problems, envy/jealousy	Pun	*King Arthur The Sword in the Stone*, Talbott	1
Man vs. Nature Man vs. Himself	Sweetness of hard won success, perseverance, rewards of diligence	Alliteration, Dialect, Rhyme, Symbolism	*When I Was Young in the Mountains*, Rylant	1
Man vs. God Man vs. Self Man vs. Nature Man vs. Society	Goodness and character are born through suffering. Providence. Grace	*Ready Readers* at CenterForLit website	*From the Mixed Up Files of Mrs. Basil E. Frankweiler*, Konigsburg	2
Man vs. Man Man vs. Society Man vs. Self Man vs. Providence	Selfless Love, Comparison and discussion of strength and weakness, Providence, Appearance vs. Reality	Frame, Imagery, Foreshadowing, Sensory Language	*Soup,* Robert Newton Peck	3
Man vs. Man Man vs. Self Man vs. Society Man vs. God	Sin Nature of Man, Sacrificial Love and Substitutionary Atonement, Redemption, the effects of Envy, Betrayal	Frame, Symbolism, Anthropomorphism	*Voyage of the Dawn Treader*, Lewis	4

Class	Title	Plot
1	*The Gardener*, Stewart	Lydia Grace must leave her family and live with her uncle in the city during the depression; her cheerful countenance and graciousness make her a blessing to everyone around her.
1	*Paul Revere's Ride,* Longfellow	The great American Poet Laureate tells the story of Paul Revere's famous ride to alert the Minutemen of the British soldiers' approach on the eve of the battle of Lexington & Concord in 1775.
1	*Crossing Bok Chitto,* Tingle	The friendship between an African American slave child and a Native American child facilitates a slave escape.
2	*Julius Caesar,* Shakespeare	Brutus, Cassius and the other conspirators plot and perform the assassination of Julius Caesar. They then fight with the Triumvirate for control of Rome, only to find that the ambitious spirit for which they killed Caesar dwells in their own hearts as well.
3	*At the Back of the North Wind,* MacDonald	A sickly boy journeys with the mythical North Wind to faraway lands and learns of her trustworthiness, faithfulness and love.
4	*Treasure Island,* Stevenson	Jim Hawkins, whose family is deeply in debt, discovers a pirate's treasure map and embarks on a dangerous journey to find the treasure, encountering honest men and ruffians in equal measure along the way.

Conflict	Theme	Aid/Devices	Alternate Title	Class
Man vs. Society Man vs. Man Man vs. Self	Bloom where you are planted A cheerful heart does good like a medicine	Teacher Guide at CenterForLit website	*The Friend*, Stewart	1
Man v. Man Man v. Society	Patriotism Liberty	*Teaching the Classics* basic seminar	*The Old Woman Who Named Things*, Rylant	1
Man v. Man Man v. Society	Friendship across racial boundaries; the incongruity of slavery	Teacher Guide at CenterForLit website	*Grandfather's Journey*, Say	1
Man v. Man Man v. Self Man v. Society	The wickedness of the human heart The law of sowing and reaping Tyranny Ambition Frailty	*Ready Readers* at CenterForLit website	*Mrs. Frisbee & the Rats of NIMH*, O'Brien	2
Man v. God Man v. Man	This allegory explores the problem of pain and the nature of death while depicting goodness, kindness and charity.	*Ready Readers* at CenterForLit website	*A Girl of the Limberlost*, Porter	3
Man v. Man Man v. Self	Coming of Age Shrewdness/Resourcefulness Honesty Mercy Friendship	*Ready Readers* at CenterForLit website	*The Pushcart War,* Merrill	4

Class	Title	Plot
1	*The Keeping Quilt,* Polacco	A Russian immigrant makes an heirloom quilt for her daughter out of the rag clothing of family members she's left behind.
1	*Amos & Boris,* Steig	When the mouse Amos's ship capsizes, he is rescued by the whale Boris; years later, Amos returns the favor unexpectedly.
1	*A Bargain for Frances,* Hoban	When Frances's friend Thelma takes advantage of her, Frances finds a way to get even.
2	*The Bronze Bow,* Speare	Daniel bar-Jamin, a rugged runaway who has cast his lot with the zealots, is recalled to responsibility by his grandmother's death. He must wrestle with his hatred for the Romans who occupy Israel and his growing love for his people.
3	*Huckleberry Finn,* Twain	Vagabond Huck and runaway slave Jim try to escape society by floating down the Mississippi River on a raft.
4	*Great Expectations,* Dickens	When the impoverished orphan Pip discovers that he has come into an inheritance from a mysterious benefactor, he distances himself from his humble friends and family to better himself and earn the love of the wealthy and beautiful Estella.

7th Grade

Conflict	Theme	Aids/Devices	*Alternate Title*	Class
Man v. Nature	The value of family heritage	Symbolism	*The Fool of the World and the Flying Ship,* Ransome	1
Man v. Nature	Friendship Kindness Faithfulness & Loyalty	Descriptive language	*Casey At the Bat,* retold by Polacco	1
Man v. Man Man v. Self	Deception Shrewdness Friendship Coming of Age	Audio Lecture at CenterForLit website	*Thunder Cake,* Polacco	1
Man v. Society Man v. Self Man v. God	Bitterness & its Effects The nature of forgiveness Sacrificial love Redemption	*Ready Readers* at CenterForLit website	*The Devil's Arithmetic,* Yolen	2
Man v. Sociey Man v. Man Man v. Self	Freedom & Slavery Character & Integrity Racism Pride vs. Humility Social Conventions	Classics Club DVD at CenterForLit website	*Henry V,* Shakespeare	3
Man v. Self Man v. Man Man vs. Society	Redemptive Love Pride vs. Humility Appearance vs. Reality Fear of Man; Bitterness Coming of Age; Friendship	Symbolism, imagery, allegory, foreshadowing	*Kidnapped,* Stevenson	4

Reading Roadmaps: A Literary Scope & Sequence for K-12 **161**

8th Grade

Class	Title	Plot
1	*I Have an Olive Tree,* Bunting	7 year old Greek immigrant Sophie wants a skateboard for her birthday; instead, Grandpa gives her an olive tree in their homeland.
1	*The Biggest Bear,* Ward	A young boy must rid the neighborhood of his beloved pet bear, who has become a nuisance.
1	*Letting Swift River Go,* Yolen	Visiting the inundated Swift River Valley which once was her home, Sally Jane makes peace with her drowned past.
2	*The Iliad,* Homer	Greek warrior and demi-god Achilles, embittered by King Agamemnon's ill treatment, refuses to reconcile and withdraws from the battle between the Greeks and the Trojans.
3	*The Yearling,* Rawlings	Jody must give up his childhood and embrace the responsibilities of a man when his pet fawn grows up to menace the family farm.
4	*The Hobbit,* Tolkien	Homebody Bilbo Baggins is petitioned by the wizard Gandalf to accompany a group of dwarves on a mission to burgle stolen treasure from the evil dragon Smaug.

Conflict	Theme	Aids/Devices	Alternate Title	Class
Man vs. Man	Heritage Maturity	Symbolism	*Eleanor,* Cooney	1
Man v. Nature Man v. Self Man v. Society	Manhood/Masculinity What is courage? Self-denial What is strength?	Pun, parody, irony, understatement	*Mirette On the High Wire ,* McCulley	1
Man v. Society Man v. Nature Man v. Self	The nature of time Bitterness & forgiveness Link between acceptance & peace	*Ready Readers* at CenterForLit website	*Angelo,* Macaulay	1
Man v. Man Man v. Self Man v. gods	Bitterness & its consequences Honor Pride Loyalty & Friendship	Epic Simile, *In Medias Res*	*Black Ships Before Troy,* Sutcliffe (a re-telling of the Iliad for children)	2
Man v. Nature Man v. Man Man v. Self	Coming of Age Childhood v. Manhood	Classics Club DVD at CenterForLit website	*A Connecticut Yankee in King Arthur's Court,* Twain	3
Man v. Self Man v. Man Man v. Society	Greed vs. Contentment Faithfulness, Selflessness Appearances v. Realities Strength coming from Weakness Good v. Evil	*Ready Readers* at CenterForLit website	*The House of 60 Fathers ,* Meindert de Jong	4

Class	Title	Plot
1	*Fishing In the Air*, Creech	A boy and his father go on a fishing trip and catch more than they expect.
1	*Owl Moon,* Yolen	A child experiences a family rite of passage when he goes owling with his father.
1	*All the Places to Love,* MacLachlan	A boy remembers all the places he's come to love and the people with whom they're associated, promising to share them with his new baby sister.
2	*The Aeneid*, Virgil	Aeneas flees a burning Troy and journeys with other refugees to establish a new homeland on the coast of Italy.
3	*Romeo and Juliet,* Shakespeare	Impetuous teen lovers from feuding families forsake their parents' authority when they marry secretly; disaster ensues.
4	*Frankenstein,* Shelley	Scientific genius Victor Frankenstein seeks immortality by creating life. His creature does not meet expectations. The disastrous consequences that follow force us to face questions about the nature of man, God and Nature.

Conflict	Theme	Aids/Devices	Alternate Title	Class
Man vs. Nature Man vs. Self	Family Heritage, the Nature of Time, Memory	*Ready Readers* at CenterForLit website	*Don Quixote,* Williams	1
Man vs. Nature Man vs. Self	Self-control, Patience, Coming of Age	Imagery, Simile, Metaphor	*Sir Gawain and the Green Knight,* Morpurgo	1
Man vs. Nature	Generational heritage, the value of the land, mortality	*Ready Readers* at CenterForLit website	*Albert,* Napoli	1
Man v. Society Man v. Man Man v. the gods	Providence Patriotism - superiority of national to personal vision	Epic simile, alliteration, personification, allegory, irony	*The Prince and the Pauper,* Twain	2
Man v. Man Man v. God	Consequences of bitterness, and rashness Consequences of rebellion Dangers of deception Star crossed love	Poetic devices: blank verse, pun, irony, etc.	*Merchant of Venice,* Shakespeare	3
Man v. Nature Man v. God Man v. Man	What is a human being? Creature/Creator distinction	Flashback	*Good Morning, Miss Dove,* Patton	4

Class	Title	Plot
1	*Beowulf,* picture storybook	Beowulf the Geat, hero of his people, voyages to the land of king Hrothgar, to whom he owes a family debt. There he delivers Hrothgar's people from the monster scourge Grendel.
1	*Canterbury Tales,* retold by Barbara Cohen	An introduction to the famous tales of Geoffrey Chaucer, this book includes short re-tellings of the Nun's Priest's Tale, the Pardoner's Tale, the Wife of Bath's Tale and the Franklin's Tale.
1	*The Clown of God,* DePaola	An orphan boy discovers his talent for juggling and makes a place for himself in society. When old age eventually robs him of it, he finds he still has place with God.
2	*Beowulf*	Beowulf the Geat, hero of his people, voyages to the land of king Hrothgar, to whom he owes a family debt. There he delivers Hrothgar's people from the monster scourge Grendel.
3	*Divine Comedy: The Inferno,* Dante	Genre: Epic Poetry. In his middle age, the narrator, aided by the beautiful Beatrice and guided by the wise poet Virgil, travels through hell to understand the nature, breadth and consequences of sin.
4	*Canterbury Tales,* Chaucer (selections: General Prologue, Nun's Priest's Tale, Pardoner's Tale, Knight's Tale)	A diverse group of 14th century English men and women meet on a pilgrimage to the cathedral at Canterbury. They decide to pass time along the journey with a storytelling contest.

Conflict	Theme	Aids/Devices	Alternate Title	Class
Man v. Animal/Monster, Man vs. Fate	Honor Good triumphs over evil The strength of virtue Fate	Kennings	*The Sign Painter,* Say	1
Conflicts vary, but all include Man v. Self, Man v. God	Human Nature Dangers of Pride, Greed Forgiving Debts	Allusion, irony, parody, allegory	*Chanticleer and the Fox,* Cooney	1
Man v. Society Man v. Self Man v. Nature Man v. God	Value of human life The holiness of all callings The joy of service	*Ready Readers* at CenterForLit website	*Yellow and Pink,* Steig	1
Man v. Animal/Monster, Man vs. Fate	Honor Good triumphs over evil The strength of virtue	Kennings	*Dream of the Rood* or Caedmon's *Hymn*	2
Man v. Self Man v. Man Man v. God	Fallen human nature Retributive Justice	Meter, epic simile, allegory, symbolism, allusion	*The Banquet,* Dante or *The Secret,* Petrarch	3
Every type of conflict is fully explored in this masterpiece	Human nature and its foibles The dangers of various character flaws Good triumphs over evil	Understatement, allegory, fable, irony	*Everyman,* Anonymous Medieval Drama	4

11th Grade

Class	Title	Plot
1	*The Giving Tree,* Silverstein	A chronicle of the lifelong friendship between a boy and a tree.
1	*Wilfrid Gordon Macdonald Partridge,* Fox	Wilfrid, a small boy, helps Miss Nancy, his elderly frend, find her memory.
1	*The Spider and the Fly ,* DiTerlizzi	A flattering spider entices a gullible fly into his parlor.
2	*Paradise Lost ,* Milton	The fallen angel, Lucifer, seeks revenge upon the Creator God by conducting a sneak attack on His newest creation, man.
3	*Hamlet,* Shakespeare	The noble prince of Denmark decides to avenge his father's murder, but struggles to make good on his pledge.
4	*Wuthering Heights ,* Bronte	A traveler uncovers the secret past of a wild and violent landowner, Heathcliff, and his one time beloved Kathy.

Conflict	Theme	Aids/Devices	Alternate Title	Class
Man vs. Man	Self-sacrificial love	Personification	*Always Room For One More* , Leodhas	1
Man vs. Nature Man vs. Self	The universal human experience The nature of friendship	*Ready Readers* at CenterForLit website	*The Tale of Meshka the Kvetch* , Chapman	1
Man vs. Man Man vs. Self	Dangers of flattery/pride	Anthropomorphism	*Song of the Swallows* , Politi	1
Creature vs. Creator, Man vs. man	The Fall of Man Origins of Sin	Epic Simile, Epic devices	*Lycidas,* Milton	2
Man vs. Himself Man vs. Fate Man vs. Man	Human frailty The Tragic Hero Sanity vs. Insanity Revenge	Classics Club DVD at CenterForLit website	*Henry V,* Shakespeare	3
Man vs. Man Man vs. Society	Perverse love/Selfish love The nature of passion Revenge/Bitterness/Betrayal Manipulation Social Prejudice	Gothic Romance, symbolism, imagery	*The Dubliners* , Joyce	4

Class	Title	Plot
1	*Emily,* Bedard	A curious child chronicles her relationship with her introverted neighbor, the poet Emily Dickinson.
1	*The Man Who Walked Between the Towers,* Gerstein	True life narrative of the French tightrope artist who walked a wire strung between the historic twin towers.
1	*The Wall,* Sis	A Czechoslovakian boy grows up in a communist state.
2	*The Red Badge of Courage*, Crane	Young and naïve Henry joins the Union Army with visions of valour and heroism, but finds such valor impossible in a world without universal truth and meaning.
3	Hemingway Unit: *The Old Man and the Sea,* "Today Is Friday," "A Clean, Well-Lighted Place"	An old Cuban fisherman, Santiago, fallen on hard luck, hooks the largest fish of his career only to have it consumed by sharks before he can bring it to shore.
4	*To Kill A Mockingbird*, Lee	Two children, Scout and Jem, become both witnesses and victims to social bigotry and racism when their father, a court appointed lawyer, defends an innocent black man accused of raping a white woman.

Conflict	Theme	Aids/Devices	Alternate Title	Class
Man vs. Society	Reclusiveness/Shyness Quiet Joy Friendship	Rhythm, metaphor, alliteration, simile, personification	*My Uncle Emily*, Yolen	1
Man vs. Society Man vs Nature	Dreams/Visions Daring	Alliteration	*So Few Of Me*, Reynolds	1
Man vs. Society Man vs. Man Man vs. Nature	Freedom vs. Tyranny, the triumph of the human spirit	Imagery	*The Three Golden Keys*, Sis	1
Man vs. Nature Man vs. Man Man vs. Self Man vs. Society	Mechanization of man Brutality of war The importance of empathy Determinism	Symbolism, imagery, metaphor, simile	*The Open Boat*, Crane	2
Man vs. Nature Man vs. Himself Man vs. Fate	Grace under pressure Empathy Disinterestedness of nature Courage in the face of a meaningless world	Symbolism, allusion	*The Pearl*, Steinbeck or *Of Mice and Men*, Steinbeck	3
Man vs. Man Man vs. Society Man vs. Himself	Lost innocence Coming of Age Self-Sacrifical Love Racial Prejudice Source of Virtue/Honor	Symbolism, allusion, simile, metaphor	*The Call of the Wild*, London	4

Chapter 6

Writing From Literature

Writing From Literature

Writing is the logical extension of the oral discussions that form the heart of the *Teaching the Classics* method. While it is not necessary that students write about every single book they read, periodic essay assignments are a crucial part of a complete literary education.

The Socratic List included in the Teaching the Classics syllabus provides dozens of excellent essay topics. Because questions on the list for each element of fiction proceed from simple to complex, essay assignments may be given to students at any reading level. Teachers can simply choose a relevant question from the list (a question, for example, that they have just finished discussing) and ask the student to summarize the discussion in writing.

Depending upon the age and ability of your students, you may also choose writing assignments such as the following:

Elementary Level:

- Three point paragraphs on the plot of the story, which may be expanded into three paragraph essays as the student matures.
- 1-3 paragraph "Key thought outline" summaries as described in Unit III of IEW's *Excellence in Writing* Program.
- Paragraph-long descriptions of the author's use of particular literary devices such as alliteration or imagery.

Junior High Level:

- 3-5 paragraph "Key thought outline" summaries (narratives) as described in Unit III of IEW's *Excellence in Writing* Program.
- Critiques as described in Unit IX of IEW's *Excellence in Writing* Program
- Page-long answers to questions from the "Theme" section of the Socratic List

High School Level:

- 2-3 page discussions of questions from the "Theme" section of the Socratic List.
- 2-3 page discussions of the author's use of literary devices, and how they relate to the other aspects of the story, such as characterization and theme.
- "Compare and contrast" exercises dealing with the characters in a particular work.
- A critical research essay that advances an argument about the story's theme which is supported not only by evidence from the text but also by the work of other interpreters. Citations and footnotes required.

The Analytical Essay

A literary analysis essay has some important structural features with which it pays to be acquainted. Here's a summary:

The Thesis

A literary essay is an argument for the essayist's interpretation of a story. The essayist states this interpretation in a very limited, very specific sentence called the thesis statement. The rest of the essay will be written to prove the truth of this statement. It is therefore crucial that the thesis be clear, arguable and unambiguous. The thesis is located at the end of the essay's first paragraph (the thesis paragraph).

Thesis paragraph

The thesis paragraph should begin with a relatively broad statement of the essay's topic that makes a claim on the reader's interest. It should then give some context for the essay's argument, narrowing its focus to a specific area of the topic. Finally, the thesis paragraph should end with the thesis statement itself. Since it proceeds from general to specific (or broad to narrow), it is helpful to think of a thesis paragraph as an inverted triangle (see diagram on the following page).

Body or Argument paragraphs

The body of the essay consists of two or more paragraphs laying out evidence for the truth of the thesis. Each paragraph contains two elements:

- Textual evidence in support of the thesis (either direct quotes or references to the text)
- Interpretation by the essayist explaining exactly how this evidence supports the thesis.

Each body paragraph presents no more than ONE argument or idea in support of the thesis. The number of arguments developed by the essayist determines the number of body paragraphs the essay should contain. Skilled essayists often arrange their arguments in a logical order with the strongest at the end for maximum rhetorical effect.

Conclusion paragraph

The conclusion of a literary essay should accomplish TWO goals:

- Restate the thesis
- Suggest implications of the thesis

The conclusion should begin with a simple restatement of the essay's argument, though not necessarily in the same words as were used in the thesis paragraph. It should then proceed to explain why the thesis is significant to the topic and what its consequences are for readers interested in the topic. Finally, it should make a broad, general statement about the topic, locating the argument and its consequences in a larger context. Since it proceeds from specific to general (or narrow to broad), it is helpful to think of a conclusion paragraph as an upright triangle, or a mirror image of the thesis paragraph (see diagram below).

The "Tootsie-Roll" Diagram

Students can remember the basic parts of a literary essay by putting these three images together to form a "Tootise-Roll," as follows:

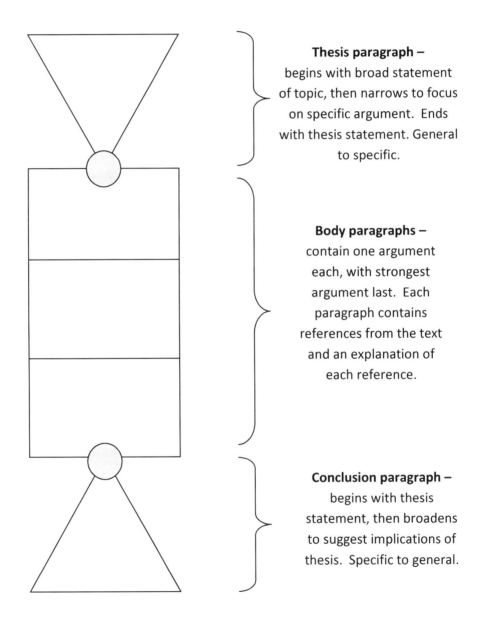

Thesis paragraph – begins with broad statement of topic, then narrows to focus on specific argument. Ends with thesis statement. General to specific.

Body paragraphs – contain one argument each, with strongest argument last. Each paragraph contains references from the text and an explanation of each reference.

Conclusion paragraph – begins with thesis statement, then broadens to suggest implications of thesis. Specific to general.

On the following page is an example of an essay using these components in an analysis of Lynd Ward's classic children's story *The Biggest Bear*. This essay was written in response to questions 11a and 13a from the Socratic List: *"Is the protagonist changed in his mind or heart by the events of the story? Does the story seem to deal with a universal theme?"*

Model Essay: *The Biggest Bear* by Lynd Ward

Surely the "coming-of-age" theme is one of classic literature's most powerful devices. When the main character of a story undergoes the painful process of maturing from a child into an adult, the reader is compelled to walk that road with him, vicariously participating in one of the most human of all dramas. In *The Biggest Bear*, protagonist Johnny Orchard completes a three-step coming-of-age process, allowing author Lynd Ward to make a profound statement about the nature of manhood.

> **Broad opening statement**

> **Limited, specific thesis statement**

As the story opens, Johnny Orchard displays a boy's obsession with his own reputation. The fact that his family grows apples instead of hunting bears galls him, and he is cut to the quick every time a neighbor comes home with a bear skin. He is especially uncomfortable when his grandfather runs from a bear instead of shooting it:

> **Argument #1**

> He was very humiliated. "If I ever see a bear," he said, "I'll shoot him so fast he won't know what hit him. And we'll have the biggest bear skin in the whole valley."

> **Direct quote from text with explanations**

Johnny is clearly desperate to be thought of as manly. Equally clear is that his idea of masculinity amounts to shooting, fighting and conquering. We can also see his self-absorption in this episode. After all, who can ever be humiliated for the sake of someone else?

As Johnny's relationship with his pet bear develops, his character develops as well. He becomes concerned with the welfare of someone besides himself. Johnny goes to great lengths to shield the bear

> **Argument #2**

from the wrath of his neighbors, taking it East, West and South into the woods to live "like other bears." His reasons for these efforts are still quite selfish; you might say that he strives to save his own pet for his own use. Nevertheless, he is not the same person who vowed to kill the first bear he laid eyes on. Instead, his eyes are turned ever so slightly away from himself.

At the climax of the story, Johnny completes the coming-of-age transformation by denying his own selfish interests altogether and freely choosing a man's responsibilities:

> *"They decided there was only one thing left to do. Johnny said he would do it."*

In volunteering to shoot the bear, Johnny denies his own wishes so that his neighbors, who have been his primary antagonists, can prosper. He lays down his life, so to speak, for the good of his friends. Johnny comes to a brand new understanding of manhood. It lies not in conquest, he finds, but in self sacrifice.

Protagonist Johnny Orchard undergoes a coming of age transformation in *The Biggest Bear* - and as he does, author Lynd Ward suggests that being a man is more complicated than it appears. Though this story was written for small children, it nevertheless deals with timeless themes common to many great works of literature. No matter how simple the story, the presence of such eternal themes always has the power to move us, and it encourages us to contemplate our own humanity. In this way, classic literature is one of the best aids to a good life.

Reference to text with explanations

Argument #3

Direct quote from text with explanations

Restatement of thesis

Broad statement of implications of thesis

Grading Literary Analysis Essays

You can grade each component of the paper separately on the 5-point scale:

- Clear thesis – 5 pts.
- Relevant supporting material – 5 pts.
- Good structure/organization – 5 pts.
- Correct grammar/mechanics – 5 pts.
- Engaging style – 5 pts.
- Total = 25 pts.

Dividing the sum of these points by 5 yields a 5-point scale grade for the entire paper. Dividing by 25 yields a percentage grade. For more information on assigning grades, see chapter 7 below, "Grading and Credits."

Lit papers should go through at least one edit. Make papers due in rough draft form 2 weeks after the class discussion, and the final draft due after 3 weeks. This will allow you to return graded final papers at the next class meeting.

_____

_____

_____

_____

_____

_____

_____

_____

_____

_____

_____

_____

Chapter 7

Learning Objectives by Grade Level

Kindergarten Literature Objectives

Students will:

-develop auditory skills - participate in hearing a story

-use good listening manners

-anticipate that written texts will have meaning

-participate in oral story telling when repetitive devices are used, supplying the text orally when appropriate

-begin to narrate back stories – story sequencing comprehension

-develop ability to interact with the story in a group – discussion skills – listening manners

-ask questions associated with story

-answer auditory questions associated with story

-identify setting, characters, problem, solution

-recognize literary devices centered around sound: alliteration, rhyme, onomatopoeia

-recognize sensory language

-identify the front cover, back cover, and title page

-hold book correctly

-follow text top to bottom, left to right

-connect auditory story with written word (symbol recognition)

-respond to stories by drawing pictures

1st Grade Literature Objectives

Students will:

-develop auditory skills - participate in hearing a story

-use good listening manners

-anticipate that written texts will have meaning

-participate in story telling when repetitive devices are used, supplying the text when appropriate

-narrate back stories – story sequencing comprehension

-develop ability to interact with the story in a group – discussion skills – listening manners

-ask questions associated with story

-answer auditory questions associated with story

-identify setting, characters, problem, solution

-identify main idea of the story – simple plot

-recognize literary devices centered around sound: alliteration, rhyme, onomatopoeia

-recognize sensory language

-identify the front cover, back cover, and title page

-follow text top to bottom, left to right

-connect auditory story with written word (symbol recognition)

-respond to stories by drawing pictures

-dictate story to correlate with drawings

-read and listen for information and pleasure

-develop reading vocabulary through listening to oral story

-develop vocabulary for future literary analysis by learning terms: protagonist, antagonist, character, plot, exposition, rising action, conflict, climax, denouement, conclusion, theme

2nd Grade Literature Objectives

Students will:

-identify the genre of books

-develop ability to predict and infer based on imbedded textual clues

-narrate through paraphrasing

-reflect on story elements to arrive at theme

-identify the link between conflict and thematic ideas

-identify important story events, discriminate non-important events

-develop independent reading habits

-grow in their ability to read orally with proper inflection and vocal modulation, expression

-develop confidence and fluency reading

-choose reading material appropriate to their reading abilities

-identify and name literary devices like rhythm, assonance, consonance, alliteration, rhyme, and sensory language

-provide description of characters

-converse about story elements one on one and in a group discussion

-grow in ability to identify thematic ideas and see their connection to conflict/resolution

-understand story frames

-understand repetition as a poetic device

-demonstrate an understanding of the difference between fiction and non-fiction

-read independently for sustained periods of time

-give oral book reports twice yearly

3rd Grade Literature Objectives

In addition to meeting the K-2nd grade objectives, students will:

-make inferences from a story

-draw conclusions from a narrative

-distinguish between literal and figurative meanings

-distinguish between genres: non-fiction, biography, fiction (sci-fi, fantasy, mystery, etc.)

-demonstrate understanding through discussion, writing, and dramatization

-begin to identify common themes from story to story (syntopical reading)

-raise questions and offer ideas about narratives

-report on 2 books read independently

-demonstrate understanding of story structure through proficiency in creating plot charts

-identify point of view from which story is told

-begin to identify literary devices such as flashback, imagery, foreshadowing, metaphor, simile, and symbolism

-begin to keep a reading journal to track their reading – including story charts, single sentence plot summaries and author information.

4th Grade Literature Objectives

In addition to meeting all the objectives for K-3 grade literature classes, students will:

-analyze major characters within a story

-trace character motives through story

-compare and contrast characters within a story

-continue their study of literary devices with irony, hyperbole, imagery, and anthropomorphism

-continue their study of genre with parody, fairytale, and historical fiction

-develop their ability to identify thematic ideas within a story, noting their universality

-continue to build their reading journal

5th Grade Literature Objectives

In addition to meeting the K-4th grade objectives, students will:

-recognize symbolism and extended metaphor

-learn about Shakespearean English and blank verse

-learn about 5 act plays

-further study story frames

-recognize elements of allegory (as in the Narnia Tales)

-identify the pourquoi story (*Why Mosquitoes Buzz in People's Ears*, e.g.)

-begin to recognize recurring plot lines in literature

-intelligently discuss the merits of good reading

-demonstrate understanding of literal and figurative meaning

-understand folktale and fairytale, and recognize it in literature

-paraphrase and summarize complex passages

-continue their reading journal

-begin to recognize famous authors and their historical eras

-present four oral book reports

6th Grade Literature Objectives

In addition to mastering the K-5th grade objectives, students will:

-begin to notice the internal consistency of a story (logic, believability, scope, implications)

-broaden understanding of allegory

-deepen understanding of figurative language and metaphor

-broaden understanding of place of myth and fairytale in fantasy literature

-understand narrative poetry

-demonstrate grasp of poetic devices including: rhyme, meter, alliteration, assonance, consonance, onomatopoeia, metaphor, simile, imagery, extended metaphor, symbolism, and allusion

-demonstrate understanding of the importance of context in understanding literature

-identify Machiavellian characters in Shakespearean literature

-demonstrate proficient ability to identify thematic ideas in a text

-write four reviews of books read independently

-begin to write expository and descriptive essays about elements from books read and discussed in class

-continue to build a reading journal/notebook

7th Grade Literature Objectives

In addition to mastering K-6th reading objectives, students will:

-recognize updated fables

-broaden grasp of extended metaphor and symbolism

-discuss elements of the epic

-develop familiarity with Homeric literature

-discuss the Trojan War cycle

-understand political allegory

-recognize social commentary in fiction

-broaden understanding of irony (verbal, circumstantial)

-understand the literary foil

-recognize and discuss philosophical naturalism in story

-recognize components of short story

-recognize recurrent themes in literature

-continue to build a reading journal

-study the lives and times of authors with an eye to understanding social context of literature.

-create new section in reading journal with author information

-recognize tone of literature

-make inferences from the text and communicate them in writing

-write persuasive essays about stories read

-write compare/contrast essays about stories read

-discuss inferences and ideas drawn from thematic elements of story in a group setting

8th Grade Literature Objectives

In addition to mastering the objectives K-7, students will:

-acquire familiarity with Arthurian legends and legend as genre

-expand familiarity with Homeric literature and devices

-recognize recurrent themes in literature. Compare and contrast thematic content between novels (syntopical reading)

-understand the elements of characterization

-intelligently define a classic

-continue their personal reading journal, expanding it to accommodate personal notes, questions, and such to encourage active reading

-continue building author identification and bio section of reading journal

-continually be required to identify authorial intention and textual integrity (internal consistency)

-utilize understanding of genre to identify author intention

-identify what a given author defines as good, true, and beautiful in a given work

-begin to grapple with thematic messages. "Is the author telling the truth as he/she understands it?"

-summarize a story or paraphrase a story

-expand a story from a summary outline

-expand story from outline, recasting setting and characters, but retaining simple plot elements

-demonstrate ability to interact with thematic ideas orally and in writing

-write persuasive thematic essays throughout the year using textual quotes to support thesis

9th Grade Literature Objectives

In addition to mastering the objectives of a K-8 grade literature education, students will:

-continue their study of the classics of Western Civilization

-encounter the chivalric romance as a genre

-encounter the beginnings of modern novel as genre

-intelligently discuss and identify parody in literature and its uses

-grapple with thematic ideas probing what it means to be human

-deepen their ability to recognize contextual elements in search of authorial intention (*The Aeneid*)

-deepen understanding of the interrelationship of setting and theme

-continue their personal reading journals

-write thematic essays on given works

-interact in classroom discussion around elements of story and thematic ideas

-begin to compare author ideas with own (i.e. "Is the author telling the truth as he/she understands it to be? Do I agree with the author?")

-begin comparative worldview analysis through literature

-track worldview/philosophy of authors in reading journal

-NOTE: Though a formal treatment of poetry is beyond the scope of this manual, high school students should be exposed annually to the structure, style and history of this important genre of literature. By the time they graduate, they should be familiar with representative works of poetry from the 16th through 20th centuries. Please contact CenterForLit for more information about incorporating poetry into your scope & sequence.

10th Grade Literature Objectives

In addition to growing proficiency with the K-9 grade objectives, students will:

-begin a new section in their reading journals entitled Literary Eras. This will track literary periods and summarize social, political, and religious issues of each

-learn literary devices associated with early English literature

-understand the importance of the use of the vernacular in literature

-understand the relationship between the written word and the development of language

-encounter the genre of the detective novel

-encounter spiritual biography as a genre

-encounter political satire as a genre

-recognize the apology as genre

-revisit epic poetry

-encounter spiritual/philosophical fantasy as a genre

-show increasing depth of proficiency in discussion of the elements of story and thematic ideas

-demonstrate growing ability to identify and discuss thematic ideas through the written essay, supporting opinions and assertions with appropriately chosen textual quotes

-demonstrate growing knowledge of famous authors and their works

-NOTE: Though a formal treatment of poetry is beyond the scope of this manual, high school students should be exposed annually to the structure, style and history of this important genre of literature. By the time they graduate, they should be familiar with representative works of poetry from the 16th through 20th centuries. Please contact CenterForLit for more information about incorporating poetry into your scope & sequence.

11th Grade Literature Objectives

In addition to K-10 literary objectives, students at this level will:

-study the field of British Lit

-become familiar with the travelogue

-revisit satire

-revisit the epic form and Milton's contribution to it

-identify romanticism as a genre and a philosophy, and identify the Romantic Period of literature and its recurrent characteristics

-encounter the Gothic Romance as a genre

-recognize the novel of manners as a late 18th and early 19th century literary genre

-revisit allegory as genre

-demonstrate increasing ability to discuss authorial intention and thematic implications of literature read

-demonstrate increasing ability to interact in the Great Conversation with authors through the written persuasive essay

-write thematic essays using textual quotes as well as noted scholars' critical analyses to support thesis

-NOTE: Though a formal treatment of poetry is beyond the scope of this manual, high school students should be exposed annually to the structure, style and history of this important genre of literature. By the time they graduate, they should be familiar with representative works of poetry from the 16th through 20th centuries. Please contact CenterForLit for more information about incorporating poetry into your scope & sequence.

12th Grade Literature Objectives

In addition to mastering and growing in the defined K-11th grade objectives, students at this level will:

-study the American authors (novelists, naturalists, essayists)

-encounter the social essay

-trace the emergence of the genre of the short story

-trace the emergence of humanistic naturalism in the 20th c.

-identify 20th century modernism as a literary period and note its philosophical presuppositions

-identify American Southern Gothic fiction as a genre

-demonstrate ease in the discussion of the elements of story

-demonstrate ability to articulate ideas of authors and personal opinions with grace, humility and style in discussion

-demonstrate growing ability to grapple with universal questions and philosophical ideas on paper through the analytical and critical essay

-continue their personal reading journals completing the literary periods section and author biography section and demonstrating active reading in their story notes

-demonstrate familiarity with a chronological timeline of literary development

-demonstrate familiarity with the ideas and movements within each literary period

-demonstrate familiarity with the classics of Western Literature and their authors

-NOTE: Though a formal treatment of poetry is beyond the scope of this manual, high school students should be exposed annually to the structure, style and history of this important genre of literature. By the time they graduate, they should be familiar with representative works of poetry from the 16th through 20th centuries. Please contact CenterForLit for more information about incorporating poetry into your scope & sequence.

Chapter 8

Grading and Credits

Grading and Credits

When it comes to grading, some parents and teachers have difficulty with the *Teaching the Classics* method because of its focus on oral instead of written work. In addition, those applying the method according to the Quarterly or Seasonal models often wonder how to assign high school credit in a situation where their students are not meeting regularly. It will therefore be helpful to explain how to grade and quantify student performance in the *Teaching the Classics* method.

The 5 point scale

We recommend a 5-point scale for evaluating student work, corresponding to the letter grades A, B, C, D and F, as follows:

1 (F)	2 (D)	3 (C)	4 (B)	5 (A)
Unacceptable	Weak	Average	Strong	Excellent

Since most *Teaching the Classics* assignments involve several elements (see below), it is easy to create an overall "points possible" grade by combining 5-point components. Also, if one component of a particular assignment needs to be weighted more heavily, a teacher can simply include that 5-point segment twice when computing the grade.

Grading Formal Discussions

Student performance in a *Teaching the Classics* discussion is affected by three factors:

- Preparation – reading the assigned materials closely before class
- Attention – following the discussion actively, regardless of participation
- Participation – making thoughtful contributions to the discussion

Grading each factor separately on the 5-point scale yields a total of 15 points possible for a discussion, and allows the teacher to consider the individual student's strengths and weaknesses in isolation. Here's an example of a grade sheet for a *Teaching the Classics* discussion:

Literature Grade Sheet				Student Name *Johnny Appleseed*	
Title	Preparation	Attention	Participation	Total	Possible
Huckleberry Finn	4	4	3	11	15
Captains Courageous	5	4	4	13	15
To Kill a Mockingbird	3	3	2	8	15

Grading Unsupervised Reading

While the teacher conducts formal discussions on the titles listed in the chosen Model (Monthly, Six-week, Quarterly, Seasonal, etc.), the student should ideally complete a larger booklist on his own. If the principles of the *Teaching the Classics* method are followed in formal discussions, this unsupervised reading will be quite profitable, as the student will inevitably apply the techniques of analysis he has learned in discussion to the books he reads in private.

Teachers may weight unsupervised reading as desired, but a good rule of thumb is to assign a single 5-point grade for the timely completion of each book on the unsupervised reading list. Award fewer points if the reading is not completed on time. Unsupervised reading can be incorporated into the grade sheet by adding a column, as follows:

Literature Grade Sheet				Student Name *Johnny Appleseed*		
Title	(Completed)	Preparation	Attention	Participation	Total	Possible
Huckleberry Finn		4	4	3	11	15
Captains Courageous		5	4	4	13	15
To Kill a Mockingbird		3	3	2	8	15
Wuthering Heights	5				5	5
Beowulf	4				4	5
The Aeneid	5				5	5
TOTAL					46	60

In this chart, the student has earned 46 out of a possible 60 point on six books, three of which were formally discussed and the other three read privately.

Grading Written Essays

Each component of an assigned essay can be evaluated on the 5-point scale as follows:

- Clear thesis – 5 points
- Relevant supporting evidence – 5 points
- Coherent structure – 5 points
- Correct grammar and syntax – 5 points
- Engaging style – 5 points

Essay grades can be incorporated into the grade sheet by adding the following columns:

Literature Grade Sheet

Student Name: Johnny Appleseed

Title	Reading (Completed)	Discussions			Essays					Totals	
		Preparation	Attention	Participation	Thesis	Supports	Structure	Grammar	Style	Total	Possible
Huckleberry Finn		4	4	3						11	15
Captains Courageous		5	4	4						13	15
To Kill a Mockingbird		3	3	2						8	15
Wuthering Heights	5									5	5
Beowulf	4									4	5
The Aeneid	5									5	5
Huck Finn					5	4	3	5	4	21	25
Beowulf					4	4	5	3	4	20	25
The Aeneid					5	5	4	3	3	20	25
									TOTAL	107	135

For more suggestions on grading literary essays, see Chapter 5 above, "Writing From Literature."

Assigning a grade for the course

A *Teaching the Classics* course grade should take into account the three components explained above: Unsupervised Reading, Formal Discussions and Written Essays. The teacher can simply compute the total points earned on the Literature Grade Sheet as a percentage of the total points possible and assign a letter grade based on that percentage:

90-100%   A

80-90%   B

70-80%   C

60-70%   D

0-60%   F

Assigning high-school credit for a *Teaching the Classics*-based literature course

High School credit is based on daily contact hours over the course of a semester or a whole year. Many high schools award a single credit for a class that meets every day for an entire school year, while others award a credit per semester for such a course. In either case, the school is awarding credit based on 5 contact (in-class) hours per week.[3]

Most teachers following the *Teaching the Classics* method do not meet their courses every day. Nevertheless, students in these courses often do the same amount of work (and certainly learn as much!). For this reason, *Teaching the Classics* does not distinguish between in-class hours and hours spent studying between classes. In our view, both activities qualify for equal credit and should be counted as contact hours.

To calculate credit in the Teaching the Classics program, therefore, teachers should count the hours their students are expected to spend reading PLUS the hours spent in formal discussion over the course of the term (whether year or semester). If this total equals or exceeds 5 hours per week, the student should be awarded full credit for the course. If the total is less than 5 hours per week, the student should be awarded that fraction of full credit. Note that this total should include not only time spent on the books covered in formal discussions, but also time spent on books assigned but not discussed.

---

[3] At the college level, since not all courses meet every day, credit is often calculated based on the number of times a course meets per week for the semester. A class that meets every day would thus count for 5 semester hours of credit, while a Monday/Wednesday/Friday course would count for 3 semester hours.

Literature Grade Sheet

Student Name: **Term:**

Title	Reading	Discussions		Essays				Totals	
	(Completed)	Preparation	Attention	Participation	Thesis	Supports	Structure	Grammar	Style	Total	Possible
TOTAL											

Chapter 9

Major Historical Periods
in Western Literature

Major Periods in Western Literature

In the broadest terms, English language literature has undergone eight major periods or movements since ancient times. They are usually described as follows (with very rough dates in parentheses):

- **Ancient** (to 500 A.D.), the literature of the Ancient Near East, Greece and Rome;

- **Medieval** (500 – 1500 A.D.), beginning with the fall of Rome and continuing until the Renaissance;

- **Renaissance** (1500 – 1660), ending with the Restoration of Charles II;

- **Neo-classical** (1660 – 1800), beginning with the Restoration and continuing through the end of the revolutionary period, when it was known as the "Age of Enlightenment";

- **Colonial American** (1620 – 1800), beginning with the Mayflower Compact and continuing through the American constitutional period.

- **Romantic** (1800 – 1865), beginning in the last decades of the 18th century and continuing through the middle of the 19th;

- **Realist** (1840 – 1914), beginning in England with the accession of Queen Victoria and in America after the Civil War, and continuing up to WWI; and

- **Modern** (1900 – 1945), running from the turn of the twentieth century to the end of WWII.

Each of these labels reflects a system of broad assumptions about the world that was more or less generally accepted by thinkers of the period. Familiarity with these assumptions can help you place the books you read in the proper historical and philosophical context. If you know what characteristics generally apply to works of Realism, for example, you'll have a clue about Mark Twain's attitude toward his subject even before you read *Huckleberry Finn*.

Two Important Cautions

Thinking in terms of literary periods is a powerful way to understand literature. However, it is not as simple as it sounds at first. Two main cautions are necessary:

Sub-periods

Within each literary period, there are variations that allow for the identification of distinct movements. *Elizabethan*, for example, is a special category of late *Renaissance* literature that includes William Shakespeare but excludes Thomas More, while the label *Victorian* corresponds to a particular kind of 19th century English *Realism* that includes Charles Dickens but not Mark Twain. It is helpful to remember that categorizing something is itself a work of interpretation, and there are as many ways to do it as there are interpreters. This guide will stick to the broadest and most generally agreed upon labels.

Overlap

New literary periods don't begin and end all at once, of course. Assumptions and conventions change gradually and unevenly, depending upon time, place and personality. The governing ideas of one period often linger long into the next, informing and shaping its development. This means that it is sometimes difficult to assign definitive dates to a particular period. For example, we can date the beginning of the Victorian period very specifically: 1837, when Victoria rose to the throne of England. It is more difficult to say exactly when Realism became the dominant mode of English literature.

Also, the fact that an author lived in a particular period doesn't necessarily mean his work bows to the conventions of that period. Literary history is full of examples of authors whose work foreshadowed future developments, or hearkened back to days gone by. Emily Bronte's *Wuthering Heights*, for example, though written in the Victorian period, has much in common with works of the Romantic period which came before. By the same token, the works of Jane Austen seem to foreshadow the Victorian age, even though they were written during the height of Romanticism.

In the end, it is best to use your understanding of literary periods as a collection of "hints" about the world view assumptions of great authors. It can be a great way quickly to explain the differences between Jack London and Nathaniel Hawthorne, for example, and pave the way for deeper study of their individual careers.

Sources

Reference texts such as the Norton Anthologies are excellent sources for information on literary periods and worldviews. In addition, they contain sizable excerpts from important works in each period. In many cases, texts are included in their entirety. In our view these volumes are worth owning as they provide an invaluable survey of Western literature.

The Norton Anthology of English Literature, 5th ed. (New York: Norton, 1986)

The Norton Anthology of American Literature, 2nd ed. (New York: Norton, 1985)

How To Use This List:

This list provides a summary of assumptions and themes common to literary works from each of the periods mentioned above. In addition, we have created a list of notable authors from each period and some of their most important works. Please note that the lists are not intended to be exhaustive. Authors and works have been included in order to illustrate and provide examples of the worldviews in question. For this reason, too, we have included some works of poetry and philosophy as well as fiction.

As with all lists, it is necessary to understand the purpose of this collection before you dive in and begin assigning books. Some booklists are created for the purpose of saying, "Here's a list of books that are good for you. You can feel perfectly safe assigning any of these books to your student, regardless of his age or experience."

This is **not** that kind of list.

The titles on this list have been chosen because they represent (to one degree or another) major worldview trends in Western thought. They will provide your students with the opportunity to engage with worldviews other than their own. *You may find the content of some of these titles disturbing or offensive – in many cases, their first readers felt the same way.*

This is especially true of the modernist period, which arose because authors felt disconnected from traditional morality and traditional world views. As a result, you will find little support for traditional morality in modernist literature! Do not expect to find it – do not be surprised if you find the opposite instead. If you are looking to Ernest Hemingway to encourage and support your students in a Christian way of thinking, you are looking in the wrong place.

If, however, your student is ready to try his hand at interpretation of the world's most influential literature and to practice taking every thought captive to the obedience of Christ, the books in this appendix are just what you need!

I. Ancient Literature (to 500)

Ancient literature is a vast category, encompassing the oral and written record of at least four civilizations: the ancient Near East, Egypt, Greece and Rome. No simple summary can hope to do justice to this body of literature. The few major works of ancient literature mentioned in Reading Roadmaps (Homer's *Iliad* and *Odyssey* and Virgil's *Aeneid*) reflect some important themes common to Greek and Roman writers, and are included to give the student a taste for the ancient classics. Teachers wishing to emphasize the ancients will find the works of the following Greek and Romans authors of interest:

Greeks (chronological):

Homer (8th century B.C.)
Hesiod (fl. 633 B.C.)
Sappho (7th century B.C.)
Archilochus (fl. 650 B.C.)
Callinus (7fl. 650 B.C.)
Tyrtaeus (fl. 640 B.C.)
Solon (b. c 640 B.C.)
Alcaeus (b. c 620 B.C.)
Semonides (7th century B.C.)
Alcman (7th century B.C.)
Stesichorus (7th century B.C.)
Mimnermus (7th century B.C.)
Aesop (620?-560? B.C.)
Thales (c. 600 B.C.)
Anacreon (fl. 550 B.C.)
Theognis (fl. 544 B.C.)
Hipponax (6th century B.C.)
Ibycus (6th century B.C.)
Simonides (b. 557/6 B.C.)
Thespis (c. 535 B.C.)
Aeschylus (524?-456 B.C.)
Pindar (518?-438? B.C.)
Bacchylides (b. c 518 B.C.)
Hecataeus (fl. 500 B.C.)
Sophocles (c. 496-406 B.C.)
Euripides (c. 485-406 B.C.)
Socrates (469?-399 B.C.)
Lysias (458-380 B.C.)
Aristophanes (c. 450-c. 385 B.C.)
Plato (429-347 B.C.)
Herodotus (fl. 450-428 B.C.)
Thucydides (fl. 430-399 B.C.)
Xenophon (430-354 B.C.)
Demosthenes (384-322 B.C.)
Aristotle (384-322 B.C.)

Diphilus (4th C B.C.)

Menander (c.342- c.292 B.C.)

Romans (alphabetical):

Ammianus Marcellinus (330 - 391 AD)

Appian (90 - 160 AD)

Apuleius (Lucius Apuleius) (125 - 171 AD)

Arrian (Flavius Arrianus) (96 - 180 AD)

Athenaeus (Athenaeus of Naucratis) (ca. AD 200)

Caesar (100 - 44 BC)

Cato the Elder(Marcus Porcius Cato) (234 - 149 BC)

Catullus (87 - 54 BC)

Cicero (Marcus Tullius Cicero) (106 - 43 BC)

Columella (Lucius Junius Moderatus Columella) (1st cent. A.D.)

Dio Cassius (Cassius Dio Cocceianus) (155 - 235? AD)

Dio Chrysostom (Dio Cocceianus Chrysostomus) (ca40 - 120 AD)

Diodorus Siculus (90 - 21 BC)

Dionysius of Halicarnassus (60/55 - 7 BC)

Eusebius (260 - 339 AD)

Eutropius (Flavius Eutropius) (4th century AD)

Florus (Lucius Annaeus Florus) (during reign of Hadrian)

Frontinus (Sextus Julius Frontinus) (40 - 104 AD)

Fronto (Marcus Cornelius Fronto) (100 - 167 AD)

Galen (Claudius Galen) (129 - 199 AD)

Gellius (Aulus Gellius) (123 - 169 AD)

Herodian (170 - 240 AD)

Horace (Quintus Horatius Flaccus) (65 - 8 BC)

Josephus (37 - 100 AD)

Julian the Apostate (Emperor Flavius Claudius Julianus) (331 - 363 AD)

Juvenal (Decimus Iunius Iuvenalis) (47 - 130 AD)

Livy (Titus Livius) (59 BC - 17 AD)

Lucan (Marcus Annaeus Lucanus) (39 - 65 AD)

Lucian (120 - 180 AD)

Lucretius (Titus Lucretius Carus) (99 - 55 BC)

Marcus Aurelius (Emperor Marcus Aurelius Antoninus) (121 - 180 AD)

Martialis (Marcus Valerius Martialis) (38/41 - 100 AD)

Nepos (Cornelius Nepos) (99 - 24 BC)

Origen (Origenes Adamantius) (185 - 254 AD)

Ovid (Publius Ovidius Naso) (43 BC - 17 AD)

Pausanias (2nd Century AD)

Petronius (Petronius Arbiter) (27 BC - 66 AD)

Philo (20 BC - 45 AD)

Plautus (254–184 BC)

Pliny the Elder (Gaius Plinius Secundus) (23 - 79 AD)

Pliny the Younger (Gaius Plinius Caecilius Secundus) (62 - 113 AD)

Plutarch (50 - 125 AD)

Polybius (200 - 123 BC)

Quintilian (Marcus Fabius Quintilianus) (35 - 100 AD)
Sallust (Gaius Sallustius Crispus) (86 - 34 BC)
Seneca (Lucius Annaeus Seneca) (4 BC - 65 AD)
Seneca the Elder (Seneca the Elder) (ca.55 Bc- ca.Ad 40)
Sextus Propertius (50 BC - 2 BC)
Strabo (66 BC - 24 AD)
Suetonius (Gaius Suetonius Tranquillus) (75 - 150 AD)
Tacitus (Publius Cornelius Tacitus) (55 - 120 AD)
Tertullian (Quintus Septimius Florens Tertullianus) (160 - 230 AD)
Valerius Maximus (Valerius Maximus) (c.20 BC-c.AD 50)
Varro (Marcus Terrentius Varro) (116 - 27 BC)
Vegetius (Publius Flavius Vegetius Renatus) (c. 400 AD)
Velleius (Velleius Paterculus) (20 BC - 30 AD)
Virgil (Publius Vergilius Maro) (70 - 19 BC)
Vitruvius (Marcus Vitruvius Pollio) (c. late 1st cent BC and 1st cent. AD)

II. Medieval Literature (500-1500)

Anglo-Saxon (500-1066)

The term "Anglo-Saxon" applies to literature produced between the invasion of Celtic England by Germanic tribes in the fifth century and the conquest of England in 1066 by William the Conqueror. This literature is heavily based on the tradition of oral storytelling, and includes epic poems such as *Beowulf*. Thematically, Anglo-Saxon literature often addressed the *heroic ideal* like its ancient predecessors, though adapted to a new situation. In the Anglo-Saxon treatment, the heroic ideal was a picture of kingly behavior that reflected the basic political and social relationship of Anglo-Saxon society: the bond between a king and his warriors. The heroic ideal involved responsibility, leadership, loyalty, generosity and, above all, skill in battle. Anglo-Saxon literature existed in part to praise the heroic virtues of its kings and so secure their eternal fame.

Anglo-Saxon England was Christianized in the 7th century, a change that is evident in the literature of the period. Interestingly enough, however, it still retained pagan elements such as the heroic ideal for a time, as the new faith worked its way into the culture. Eventually, Christian themes replaced these pagan ideas and traditions, but this was a long process. Consequently, in Anglo-Saxon literature we find a mingling of Christian and pagan elements. Biblical figures like Moses, Jesus and even God the Father often appeared as Beowulf-like heroes, performing mighty deeds.

Authors: Anglo-Saxon Literature

Anonymous
The Dream of the Rood (seventh century)
Beowulf (eighth century)
The Battle of Maldon (tenth century)
Caedmon
Hymn (seventh century)

Middle English (1066 -1500)

The Norman conquest of England in 1066 marks a significant change in the development of English literature. Where Anglo-Saxon literature had been written by and for the aristocracy (that is, kings and their households), Middle English literature was popular literature, written by and for people of the lower classes.

This change had a significant effect on the subject matter of Middle English literature. Its heroes, for example, were not the idealized kings of the Anglo-Saxon period; instead, they were real human protagonists who not only fought but also laughed, cried, played games, and above all, fell in and out of love. The situations of ordinary life played a much larger part in Middle English literature than they had before 1066.

Despite its new directions, Middle English literature continued to reflect the centrality of Christianity in the medieval world. Virtually all works, whether sacred or secular, dealt with issues such as personal salvation and the institutional church. Even the courtly love tales which were popular throughout the medieval period were told from within the framework of Christian doctrines such as sin, self-sacrifice and piety.

Authors: Middle English Literature

Anonymous
Piers Plowman (c. 1372-1389)
Sir Gawain and the Green Knight (c. 1375-1400)
Everyman (after 1485)

Geoffrey Chaucer (c. 1343-1400)
The Canterbury Tales (c. 1386-1400)

Margery Kempe (1373-1438)
The Book of Margery Kempe (date unknown)

Sir Thomas Malory (c. 1405-1471)
Morte Darthur (1485)

Other Works of Medieval Literature:

III. Renaissance Literature (1500-1660)

The English Renaissance is usually dated from the accession of Henry Tudor in 1485. The literature of this period was affected by several very different movements, from Renaissance humanism and the Protestant Reformation to English nationalism, which came of age under Queen Elizabeth I (r. 1558-1603). It is notoriously difficult to define a "Renaissance worldview," but the career of Sir Philip Sydney is perhaps the best illustration. Sydney was a courtier to Elizabeth I and served her as a foreign ambassador; he was a patron of the arts and a humanist scholar in his own right; he was a poet whose Petrarchan sonnets rank among the finest in history; he was the greatest literary critic of his day; he was an earnest supporter of Protestant reform at home and abroad; and he was a famous soldier who died in battle for the cause of Protestantism. Sydney was England's greatest "Rennaissance man," whose broad interests, far reaching education, religious fervor and fierce patriotism make him a good example of the worldview of this period.

More specifically, characteristics of a Renaissance world view include the following details:

- Interest in classical (that is, Greek and Roman) learning and in the original versions of ancient texts, including those of the Old and New Testaments;

- Interest in the *studia humanitatis* (literally, the "study of things human"): language, literature, history, art and government. These subjects were seen as distinct from the medieval disciplines of theology, philosophy and law, which concerned God rather than man.   The Renaissance emphasis on these subjects is the origin of the terms *humanism* and the *humanities*. It is quite distinct from secular humanism, a 20th century social and political philosophy.

- Interest in the issue of true religion and how it should be realized in the world. This was the question of the Protestant Reformation and it had literary as well as political implications both in England and in her American colonies.

- Interest in human government and how it should be structured. This issue surfaced in a variety of Renaissance era works, from the treatises of Hobbes and Locke to the plays of Shakespeare and the sermons of the Massachusetts Bay Puritans.

Authors: Renaissance Literature

Poets
Sir Thomas Wyatt (1503-1542)
Sir Walter Raleigh (1552-1618)
John Donne (1572-1631)
George Herbert (1593-1633)
Andrew Marvell (1621-1678)

Sir Thomas More (1478-1535)
Utopia (1516)

Edmund Spenser (1552-1599)

The Shepheardes Calender (1579)

The Faerie Queene (1590, 1596)

Sir Philip Sydney (1554-1586)

Arcadia (1590)

Astrophil and Stella (1591)

William Shakespeare (1564-1616)

Hamlet (c. 1599)

Much Ado About Nothing (c. 1598)

Henry V (c. 1599)

Poems

Christopher Marlowe (1564-1593)

Dr. Faustus (1592)

Ben Jonson (1572-1637)

Volpone (1606)

The Alchemist (1610)

Poems

Thomas Hobbes (1588-1679)

Leviathan (1651)

John Milton (1608-1674)

Lycidas (1637)

Paradise Lost (1667)

Samson Agonistes (1671)

John Bunyan (1628-1688)

The Pilgrim's Progress (1675) – a Renaissance work, though written in the neo-classical period

Other Works of Renaissance Literature:

IV. Neo-classical Literature (1660 – 1800)

Some have described the period after the restoration of Charles II as "a new age of elegance" in literature. Reacting against the intricacy, flamboyance, boldness and extravagance of the late Renaissance, writers in this period tended to favor simplicity, clarity, restraint, regularity and good sense. They were interested in discovering the rules that govern the world and then working within them to produce beauty. The rules themselves often became the subject of their work, which is part of the reason for the interest in political theory throughout this period.

The neo-classical period gets its name from the fact that these writers often strove to imitate the style of ancient Roman authors like Virgil, Ovid and Horace, who wrote during the reign of Augustus Caesar in the first century AD. Neo-classical writers were also sensitive to the issues of their own day, however, and it is instructive to notice that this period in literature coincided with the development of rationalistic philosophies, the rise of experimental science and a general desire for peace and order after an era of violent religious and political extremism.

Some ideas common to many writers during the neo-classical period include:

- A negative view of the natural passions. Neo-classical authors assumed that natural passions should be subordinated to social needs and strictly controlled. The writings of Benjamin Franklin on this subject are perfectly illustrative of the neo-classical worldview. Hobbes' *Leviathan* is a good example of a Renaissance era work that foreshadowed the neo-classical period in this respect.

- A positive view of natural human reason. Perhaps because experimental science was gaining popularity, neo-classical authors began to assume that man's methodical use of his rational powers could lead him to truth in a variety of areas, whether philosophical, political or religious. Even preachers in this period demonstrated this way of thinking, as the writings of the American Jonathan Edwards illustrate.

- A search for meaning in the order of things. Neoclassical thinkers believed that the order of nature, social hierarchies, government and religion was the source of happiness and contentment. Even the order within literary forms was an end in and of itself.

- A concern for the needs of society before the needs of the individual. This idea helps explain why you see lots of constitutions and political theory in the neoclassical period, and why authors such as John Locke were so influential.

Authors: Neo-classical literature

John Locke (1632-1704)
Essay Concerning Human Understanding (1690)

Two Treatises of Government (1690)

John Dryden (1637-1700)
Absalom and Achitophel (1681)
Translation of Virgil (1697)
Poems

Daniel Defoe (1660-1731)
Robinson Crusoe (1719)

Jonathan Swift (1667-1745)
Gulliver's Travels (1726)

Alexander Pope (1688-1744)
The Rape of the Lock (1712)
Poems

Samuel Johnson (1709-1784)
Translation of Horace (1784)
Dictionary (1755)
Lives of the Poets (1781)
Poems

Other Works of Neo-classical Literature:

_____

_____

_____

_____

_____

_____

_____

_____

_____

_____

_____

V. Colonial American Literature (1620 -1800)

In many ways, American literature of the seventeenth and eighteenth centuries responded to the same intellectual and cultural currents as its English counterpart. As a result, it shares many of the characteristics of Neo-classical literature as described above. In addition, however, American authors in this period were deeply affected by the uniquely American experience of founding a new society in the wilderness. This process eventually gave rise to a new national literature in America. It is therefore customary to consider American literature separately after 1620.

Authors: Colonial American Literature

John Winthrop (1588-1649)
A Model of Christian Charity (1630)

William Bradford (1590-1657)
Of Plymouth Plantation (written 1630-1647; first published 1856)

Roger Williams (1603-1683)
The Bloody Tenet of Persecution for the Cause of Conscience (1644)

Anne Bradstreet (1612-1672)
The Tenth Muse Lately Sprung up in America (1650) – the first American poetry ever published

Cotton Mather (1663-1728)
Magnalia Christi Americana (1702)

Mary Rowlandson (c. 1637-c.1711)
Captivity Narrative (1682)

Edward Taylor (1642-1729)
Poems

Jonathan Edwards (1703-1758)
Personal Narrative (c. 1740)
Sinners in the Hands of an Angry God (1741)

Benjamin Franklin (1706-1790)
Autobiography (1771-1790, published 1791)
Poor Richard's Almanac (1732-1757)

J. Hector St. John de Crevecoeur (1735-1813)
Letters from an American Farmer (1782)

Thomas Paine (1737-1809)
Common Sense (1776)
The American Crisis (1776)
The Age of Reason (1793)

Thomas Jefferson (1743-1826)
Declaration of Independence (1776)
Notes on the State of Virginia (1785)

Other Works of Colonial American Literature:

_____

_____

_____

_____

_____

_____

_____

_____

_____

_____

_____

_____

_____

_____

_____

_____

_____

_____

_____

VI. Romantic Literature (1800 – 1865)

Romanticism as a literary movement arose in the late 18th century in the aftermath of the French Revolution. In many ways, Romanticism was a reaction against the formal, orderly literature of the neo-classical period. Its beginning is commonly associated with the publication of William Wordsworth's *Lyrical Ballads* in 1798. In England, the Romantic period ended in 1832 with the death of Sir Walter Scott, one of its most famous novelists. In America, however, the Romantic impulse continued through the Civil War – Harriet Beecher Stowe and Abraham Lincoln were both affected by Romanticism, as were many of the preachers and politicians of the antebellum period.

Romanticism is no easier to define than any other literary movement, but Romantics tended to share certain general assumptions about the world, including faith in mankind's innate goodness and eventual perfectibility. They saw men as equal at birth, individually unique and capable of infinite self-development. They stressed the value of expressing human abilities that were common to all from birth rather than from training. Romantics owed a debt to French philosopher Jean Jacques Rousseau, whose image of the noble savage became their ideal vision of humanity freed from the stifling boundaries of civilization.

Romantics in England were poets more often than not, although novelists such as Scott and Jane Austen also belong to the period. The works of Romantic authors are likely to deal with themes such as the following:

Radical individualism

Neo-classical literature had described men and women as limited beings in a strictly ordered world which changed little from generation to generation. The limits of the human species were often the subjects, not only of fiction but also of philosophy and political theory. The glory of neo-classical literature was to exult in order, precedent, long-established principles and common sense.

Romantic authors reacted strongly against this tradition, and put immense faith in the power and potential of the individual man. The individual who refuses to submit to limitations (whether of species, class, race or sex) is often the hero in Romantic fiction, because he is the true human being. Earlier ages might have called this striving sin; the Romantics called it a triumph.

Romantic works often depict characters isolated from society or at least struggling against its rules and regulations: Cain, Satan, Faust, Prometheus, Napoleon, the Ancient Mariner and Hester Prynne are good examples.

Nature

The description of scenery and natural imagery figured prominently in many works of the Romantic period. Nature was often used as a symbol of the freedom of the human soul when unfettered by the restraints imposed by society. Scenic beauty reminded Romantic authors of the possibilities of the human soul, and they used Nature as a model for harmony in the world. If we could all act according to our pure, essential natures, they argued, we would get along much better. Romantic works therefore tend to advocate the emotional, intuitive and sensual side of the human experience against the orderly, restrained demands of established human society. Hawthorne's *The Scarlet Letter* is a wonderful example of this theme in action, complete with symbolism and imagery that perfectly illustrate the Romantic faith in Nature. The novels of James Fenimore Cooper also show these assumptions very clearly.

Imagination

Among Romanticism's most characteristic traits was faith in the individual imagination and its ability to triumph over the senses. Romantic authors believed that the chief aim of life was learning to "see" the world through the imagination, and so *transcend* its troubles and difficulties. In fact, one important group of American Romantics, which included Ralph Waldo Emerson, Henry David Thoreau and Louisa May Alcott called themselves *transcendentalists*, and this belief informed their writings and philosophies. The Romantics saw a supernatural power in the individual imagination – a power strong enough literally to remake the world. By demonstrating this imagination at work in their poems and novels, they hoped to effect a revolution just as real as the ones the French and Americans had attempted in the late 18th century. The essays of Ralph Waldo Emerson, though not fiction, are important in this regard, as are the poems of William Wordsworth, Samuel Taylor Coleridge and Lord Byron.

Authors: English Romanticism

Poets
William Worsdworth (1770-1850)
Samuel Taylor Coleridge (1772-1834)
George Gordon, Lord Byron (1788-1824)
Percy Bysshe Shelley (1792-1822)
John Keats (1795-1821)

Sir Walter Scott (1771-1832)
Rob Roy (1817)
The Heart of Midlothian (1818)
Ivanhoe (1819)

Jane Austen (1775-1817)
Pride and Prejudice (1813)
Sense and Sensibility (1811)
Emma (1815)
Persuasion (1817)

Mary Shelley (1797-1851)
Frankenstein (1818) – this novel belongs to a subcategory of Romantic fiction, the Gothic terror novel.

Authors: American Romanticism

Washington Irving (1783-1859)

History of New York (1809)
Sketchbook of Geoffrey Crayon (1820) – contains "Rip van Winkle" and "The Legend of Sleepy Hollow"
Tales of a Traveler (1824)

James Fenimore Cooper (1789-1851)
The Deerslayer (1841)
Last of the Mohicans (1826)
The Pathfinder (1840)
The Pioneers (1823)
The Prairie (1827)

Ralph Waldo Emerson (1803-1882)
Nature (1836)
Self-Reliance (1841)
The Over-Soul (1841)
Concord Hymn (1837)
Poems

Nathaniel Hawthorne (1804-1864)
The Scarlet Letter (1850)
The House of Seven Gables (1851)
The Blithedale Romance (1852)

Henry Wadsworth Longfellow (1807-1882)
Poems on Slavery (1842)
Evangeline (1847)
The Song of Hiawatha (1855)
Tales of a Wayside Inn (1863), includes "Paul Revere's Ride"

Edgar Allan Poe (1809-1849)
The Fall of the House of Usher (1839)
The Murders in the Rue Morgue (1841)
The Raven (1845)
A Descent into the Maelstrom (1845)
The Cask of Amontillado (1846)
Annabel Lee (1849)
The Masque of the Red Death (1850)
The Telltale Heart (1850)
The Pit and the Pendulum (1850)

Henry David Thoreau (1817-1862)
Walden (1854)
Civil Disobedience (1849)

Herman Melville (1819-1891)
Moby Dick (1851)
Billy Budd, Sailor (first published in 1924)

Harriet Beecher Stowe (1811-1896)
Uncle Tom's Cabin (1852)

Other Works of Romantic Literature:

_____

_____

_____

_____

_____

_____

_____

_____

_____

_____

_____

_____

_____

_____

_____

_____

_____

_____

_____

_____

_____

_____

V. Realist Literature (1840-1900)

The beginning of the reign of Queen Victoria (1837) is usually considered the dawn of literary Realism. This period lasted throughout the 19th century in England, and well into the 20th century in America. Just as Romanticism had been a reaction against Neo-classicism, Realism was a reaction against Romanticism. Where Romantics stressed the limitless potential of the individual imagination, Realists preferred a faithful representation of the facts. It has been said that Romantics saw the individual as a god, while Realists saw him as a common man. In any event, Realists were less concerned with human potential than with human problems.

Where Romantics looked to an ideal world free from the corruption of civilization, Realists concerned themselves with the world as it was. Their works were thus characterized by attention to the social, economic and political issues of the 19th century. These included the problems of industrialization and urbanization, as in Charles Dickens' novels about London's lower classes; the relationship between traditional religion and new philosophies such as Darwinism, as in Rudyard Kipling's descriptions of Imperial India; and the problems of poverty and inequality, as in Mark Twain's treatment of American slavery.

Where Romantics had encouraged readers to see "through" their eyes to an idealized reality beyond the senses, Realists preferred to see "with" their eyes what was actually before them. Above all, realist fiction emphasized the accurate representation of detail. A wonderful (and hilarious) example of the difference between Realism and Romanticism on this point is Mark Twain's essay entitled "James Fenimore Cooper's Literary Offenses," in which Twain evaluates the Romantic use of description from a Realist's perspective.

In England, the Realist movement took place during the reign of Queen Victoria (r. 1837-1901), and so it is known as the **Victorian period**.

Authors: Victorian Literature

Thomas Carlyle (1795-1881)
Sartor Resartus (1833-1834)
The French Revolution (1837)
The Life of John Sterling (1851)

Charles Dickens (1812-1870)
The Pickwick Papers (1836-1837)
The Adventures of Oliver Twist (1837-1839)
The Life and Adventures of Nicholas Nickleby (1838-1839)
Barnaby Rudge (1841)
A Christmas Carol (1843)
David Copperfield (1849-1850)
Bleak House (1852-1853)
A Tale of Two Cities (1859)
Great Expectations (1860-1861)

William Makepeace Thackeray (1811-1863)
Vanity Fair (1848)

George Eliot (1819-1880)
Adam Bede (1859)
Silas Marner (1861)
Middlemarch (1871-1872)

Emily Bronte (1818-1848)
Wuthering Heights (1847)

Charlotte Bronte (1816-1855)
Jane Eyre (1847)

Thomas Hardy (1840-1928)
Jude the Obscure (1895)

Rudyard Kipling (1865-1936)
Gunga Din (1890)
The Jungle Book (1894)
The Second Jungle Book (1895)
Captains Courageous (1897)
Kim (1901)

Authors: American Realism

Mark Twain (1835-1910)
The Celebrated Jumping Frog of Calaveras County (1867)
The Innocents Abroad (1869)
The Adventures of Tom Sawyer (1876)
The Prince and the Pauper (1882)
The Adventures of Huckleberry Finn (1884)
A Connecticut Yankee in King Arthur's Court (1889)
Fenimore Cooper's Literary Offenses (1895)
The Man that Corrupted Hadleyburg (1900)

William Dean Howells (1837-1920)
A Chance Acquaintance (1873)
A Modern Insurance (1882)
The Rise of Silas Lapham (1884)
Indian Summer (1885)
The Kentons (1902)

Henry James (1843-1916)
The Portrait of a Lady (1881)
The Wings of the Dove (1902)
The Absassadors (1903)
The Golden Bowl (1904)

Kate Chopin (1850-1904)
The Awakening (1889) – this novel illustrates a Romantic worldview even though it was written during the age of Realism.

Naturalism

Naturalism may be considered a distinct form of realism that lasted until the first World War. Naturalism was an extension of realism, in the sense that naturalist authors were also concerned about the real world. They focused on this world for slightly different reasons, however: many naturalists were adherents of Darwin's theory of evolution, and denied the existence of anything beyond the physical senses.

Naturalists believed that man's existence is determined entirely by blind external or biological forces such as heredity and the environment. Since most naturalist authors were atheists, their works also tended to stress the role of chance rather than Providence or Fate in determining life's outcomes. If Romantics saw the individual as a god and Realists saw him as a common man, Naturalists saw him as a helpless animal.

Naturalists often wrote about the fringes of society – the criminal, the fallen, the down-and-out – in order to draw attention to the animalistic nature of man. In many naturalist works, man shares characteristics with the animal world, and is not much better off than brute beasts when it comes to controlling his environment or his destiny.

Authors: Naturalism

Edith Wharton (1862-1937)
The House of Mirth (1905)
Ethan Frome (1912)
The Age of Innocence (1920)

Frank Norris (1870-1902)
McTeague (1899)
The Octopus (1901)
The Pit (1903)

Stephen Crane (1871-1900)
Red Badge of Courage (1895)

Theodore Dreiser (1871-1945)
Sister Carrie (1900)

Jack London (1876-1916)
To Build a Fire (1902)
The Call of the Wild (1903)
The Sea Wolf (1904)
White Fang (1906)

Other Works of Realist Literature:

_____

_____

_____

_____

_____

_____

_____

_____

_____

_____

_____

_____

_____

_____

_____

_____

_____

_____

_____

_____

_____

_____

VI. Modernist Literature (1900-1945)

The Modern period in English language literature dawned in the early 20th century as Western civilization began to undergo cataclysmic changes. These changes caused widespread feelings of disorientation, rootlessness and uncertainty. Writers of the modern period were motivated by the sense that an old world had passed away and there was nothing with which to replace it.

The ideas of Karl Marx undermined faith in 19th century models for economic and political progress. World War I had destroyed that century's geopolitical system and offered no guarantees of future stability. Dramatic innovations in technology became widely available, including telephones, radios, phonographs, moving pictures and automobiles. By making communication and transportation easier, these inventions fostered restlessness and dissatisfaction. The growth of modern science, embodied in Einstein's theory of Relativity and Darwin's theory of evolution, undermined faith in the traditional Christian explanations of natural phenomena. The social ideas of Sigmund Freud led to unsettling conclusions about traditional family relationships. Political controversies surrounding prohibition and women's suffrage added to the feeling that the whole world was turning upside down.

Modernist literature attempted to convey this sense of uncertainty and to depict a society in decay. Where the Realists of the late 19th century still held to the idea that society was something stable that could be accurately described, modernists felt forced by the events of their time to reject this assumption. At the heart of modernist literature was the conviction that the traditional structures of human life – religious, social, political, economic and artistic – had either been destroyed or proven false.

Modernist fiction reflected this conviction in its style and structure. The typical modernist story comes across as a collection of disjointed fragments. It will seem to begin arbitrarily, to advance without explanation and to end without resolution, consisting of vivid segments juxtaposed without cushioning or integrating transitions. For this reason, modernist stories such as Hemingway's *The Sun Also Rises* can be unsettling to the reader.

Modernist works are often spare of language, compressed, vivid and direct. They often portray characters who exhibit none of the traits that earlier ages would have ascribed to heroes. The protagonists in a modernist story are often aimless and defeated, frustrated in their search for meaning.

Authors: Modernism

Willa Cather (1873-1947)
O Pioneers! (1913)
My Antonia (1918)
Death comes for the Archbishop (1927)

James Joyce (1882-1941)
A Portrait of the Artist as Young Man (1916)

Ulysses (1922)
Finnegans Wake (1939)

Virginia Woolf (1882-1941
Mrs. Dalloway (1925)
To the Lighthouse (1927)
Orlando (1928)

T.S. Eliot (1888-1965)
The Love Song of J. Alfred Prufrock (1917)
The Waste Land (1922)
The Hollow Men (1925)
Ash Wednesday (1930)

F. Scott Fitzgerald (1896-1940)
The Beautiful and the Damned (1922)
This Side of Paradise (1920)
The Great Gatsby (1925)
Tender is the Night (1934)

William Faulkner (1897-1962)
The Sound and the Fury (1929)
As I Lay Dying (1930)
Light in August (1932)
Absalom, Absalom! (1936)
The Unvanquished (1938)

Ernest Hemingway (1899-1961)
The Sun Also Rises (1926)
A Farewell to Arms (1929)
Winner Take Nothing (1933)
The Snows of Kilamanjaro (1936)
To Have and Have Not (1937)
For Whom the Bell Tolls (1940)
The Old Man and the Sea (1952)

John Steinbeck (1902-1968)
Of Mice and Men (1937)
The Grapes of Wrath (1939)
The Pearl (1947)
East of Eden (1952)

Appendix

A Glossary of Literary Devices

Allegory – A figurative story, in which the principal subject is depicted by another subject resembling it in its properties and circumstances; a symbolic representation; a narrative in which abstract ideas are personified; a sustained metaphor. (i.e. *At the Back of the North Wind*, *Everyman*, *The Pilgrim's Progress*)

Antagonist – The character that impedes the progress of the protagonist towards his goal.

Anthropomorphism – A device by in which human qualities are ascribed to animals.

Anti-hero – The protagonist that fails to demonstrate the typical heroic qualities. Charlie Brown, for example.

Archetype –The original pattern after which a thing is made. A model or first form.

Bard – an oral storyteller.

Catharsis – an emotional release provided by an artistic or aesthetic experience.

Character – one of the actors in a story.

Characterization – The creative act of describing and developing a fictional character.

Climax – The turning point of a story; the highest point of interest. The peak of tension.

Close Reading – Reading a second time paying attention to details.

Comedy – A dramatic composition of light and humorous character, typically with a happy ending.

Conflict – The problem that drives the plot of a story forward toward its conclusion.

Connotation – The implied meaning given to words by the author of a story, often through the emotional weight they carry.

Context – Text surrounding words that gives those words significance; historical and cultural factors surrounding events that give those events significance.

Criticism – A philosophy of literature that encompasses well developed viewpoints on the proper way to read, understand, and interpret it.

Dénouement – The disentangling of the intricacies of the plot of a story. Also referred to as Falling Action.

Dialogue – Written conversation between two or more characters.

Dramatic Monologue – type of poem in which the poet assumes a persona and delivers a speech, either thinking out loud to himself, or his portion of a conversation with an implied listener the nature of which is revealing of his ambitions, motives, or personal character.

Epic – a long narrative poem of world-encompassing scope and universal themes that employs certain literary devices and conforms to certain poetic conventions.

Exposition – The introduction of a story, where the author presents his characters in their setting and hints at the central conflict that will drive the story forward.

Fiction – Narrative writing that is not factual. Examples include novel, short story, myth and fable.

Figurative Meaning – Meaning that lies beneath the surface. Implied meaning, serving as illustration.

Figure – A stock character within a story. Examples include the Christ-Figure, the Hero, the Villain, and the Everyman.

Foil – A character created to demonstrate the qualities of the hero through comparison and contrast.

Foreshadowing – Hints within the text of events that will take place later in the story.

Frame – The external story, or the narrative context in which the story takes place.

Genre – A type of literature, distinguished from other types by form, technique, and subject matter. Here is a list of some important genres (not a complete list by any means!):

Prose
    Fiction

Historical fiction	Fable
Science fiction	Folktale
Fantasy	Myth
Western	Legend
Romance	Adventure story
Detective story	Drama

    Non-fiction
        Encyclopedia/Almanac/Reference book

News article	Essay
Textbook	Autobiography
Biography	Philosophical treatise
Scientific treatise	History

Poetry
    Narrative

Epic	Ballad

    Lyric

Nursery rhyme	Sonnet
Haiku	Villanelle

Hero – A successful, strong protagonist; a "superman" whose virtuous qualities separate him from the other characters in a story.

Irony – A mode of speech or writing expressing a literal sense contrary to the meaning intended by the speaker.

Literal Meaning – The face value of words or ideas.

Literary Device – A verbal tool employed by an author to enhance the effect of his story. Examples include imagery, alliteration, metaphor and rhyme.

Literary Period – The historical era that was the scene of the development of a particular type of literary expression.

Motif – A theme or idea that appears repeatedly throughout a story and characterizes it.

Non-Fiction – Writing that is based in fact. Examples include biographies, news stories, encyclopedia articles, and research papers.

Novel – A long work of fiction.

Novella – A short novel.

Paradox – An apparent contradiction.

Persona – The personality assumed by a poet; the voice in which a poet speaks.

Personification – A comparison in which human qualities are assigned to inanimate things.

Plot – The sequence of events in a story; the simple story line.

Poem – A verse composition, especially one characterized by economy of linguistic expression, vivid imagery, and intense emotional tone. Generally characterized by adherence to rules of structure and form, including rhythm and sometimes rhyme.

Point of View – The perspective from which a story is told. Examples include 1st person, 3rd person narrative, 3rd person omniscient, and 3rd person limited.

Prose – Writing that is not poetry. Examples include essays, novels, and literary criticism.

Protagonist – The hero (or anti-hero) in a story; the character whose quest forms the main idea of the plot.

Pun – A play on words, often resulting in humorous effects.

Satire – The use of irony, sarcasm, or ridicule to expose, denounce or deride a particular vice or folly. A literary composition in verse or prose in which such vices or abuses are held up to scorn, derision, or ridicule.

Setting – The place and time in which the action of the story occurs.

Soliloquy – A monologue delivered by a performer alone onstage, during which he reveals his innermost thoughts to the audience, but not to the other performers.

Stock Characters – Familiar characters used regularly and interchangeably in a wide variety of stories. Examples include the young lovers, the snake oil salesman, the court jester and the stiff butler.

Symbolism – The use in literature of an object to represent something else. The object usually carries both a figurative and literal meaning. In general, a symbol is a concrete thing that stands for an abstract idea. (i.e. a flag represents the ideals of a nation, patriotism, etc.)

Theme – The underlying idea the author hopes to communicate in his story; the author's message; the leading subject upon which the author writes. (Some universal themes include: Mob Rule, Prejudice, Betrayal, Innocence, Materialism vs. Idealism, Pride and Humility, Ambition, Good vs. Evil, Coming of Age, Personal Honor, Loyalty, Survival, etc.)

Tragedy – A drama portraying the struggle of a strong-willed protagonist against fate. The downfall of the protagonist usually hinges upon the fatal flaw in his otherwise heroic character.

Voice – The tone of the author, as the product of his vocabulary and syntax.